KATE HALE

SEO Accounting

For Beginners

Copyright © 2024 by KATE HALE

All rights reserved. No part of this publication may be reproduced, stored or transmitted in any form or by any means, electronic, mechanical, photocopying, recording, scanning, or otherwise without written permission from the publisher. It is illegal to copy this book, post it to a website, or distribute it by any other means without permission.

First edition

*This book was professionally typeset on Reedsy.
Find out more at reedsy.com*

Contents

Introduction to SEO Accounting	1
Getting Started with SEO	8
Keyword Research for Accountants	17
On-Page SEO Essentials	27
Local SEO for Accountants	45
Link Building Strategies	53
SEO Tools and Resources	61
Tracking Your SEO Performance*	70
Common SEO Mistakes to Avoid	79
Advanced SEO Tactics for Accountants	88
SEO Case Studies and Success Stories	98
Developing an Ongoing SEO Strategy	107
Conclusion	118

Introduction to SEO Accounting

What is SEO Accounting?

SEO Accounting refers to the application of Search Engine Optimization (SEO) techniques to the field of accounting. It's a strategic approach that helps accountants and accounting firms increase their online visibility, attract more clients, and enhance their digital presence. In today's digital age, simply having a website isn't enough. Your potential clients are searching for accounting services online, and if your website isn't optimized to appear in search results, you're missing out on significant business opportunities.

SEO involves a set of practices aimed at improving your website's ranking on search engines like Google. By optimizing your content, website structure and external links, you can make it easier for search engines to understand and recommend your site to users. For accountants, this means more traffic to your site, more inquiries, and ultimately, more clients. SEO Accounting is about tailoring these practices to meet the specific needs of accounting professionals, ensuring that your website not only attracts visitors but converts them into clients.

The core of SEO Accounting revolves around understanding what potential clients are searching for, how search engines work, and how to align your online content with these search behaviors. This approach moves beyond traditional marketing tactics, using data-driven strategies to place your services in front of those actively seeking them. It's not just about reaching a broad audience but about connecting with the right audience — those who are most likely to need and value your services.

Why SEO is Essential for Accountants

The accounting industry, like many others, has seen a shift towards digital transformation. With this shift, competition has increased, making it more important than ever to stand out in the crowded marketplace. Here's why SEO is essential for accountants:

1. Visibility and Reach: Most people turn to search engines when looking for professional services, including accounting. If your website doesn't appear on the first page of search results, your chances of being discovered drop significantly. SEO helps improve your rankings, making it easier for potential clients to find you.

2. Credibility and Trust: Websites that rank higher on search engine results are often perceived as more credible and trustworthy. By optimizing your site with relevant content, back links, and technical elements, you not only improve your visibility but also build trust with prospective clients.

3. Cost-Effective Marketing: Compared to traditional marketing methods such as print ads or direct mail, SEO is a cost-effective strategy. It targets users who are actively searching for accounting services online, leading to higher conversion rates and a better return on investment.

4. Local SEO Advantage: For accountants, local SEO is particularly beneficial. It allows you to target potential clients in your geographical area, making it easier to connect with businesses and individuals who are nearby and in need of your services.

INTRODUCTION TO SEO ACCOUNTING

5. Long-Term Benefits: Unlike paid advertising, the results of SEO are long-lasting. Once you achieve good rankings, you can maintain them with ongoing optimization and quality content, ensuring a steady stream of potential clients over time.

6. Adapting to Consumer Behavior: Consumer behavior has shifted dramatically with the rise of digital technology. Clients now expect to find services online quickly and easily. By embracing SEO, accountants can meet these expectations, positioning themselves as accessible and client-focused.

7. Competitive Edge: Many accounting firms have yet to fully embrace SEO, meaning there's an opportunity to get ahead of competitors who are still relying on outdated marketing tactics. By adopting SEO strategies, you can differentiate your firm and capture market share.

In summary, SEO is not just an optional marketing tool; it's a necessary strategy for accountants who want to grow their business and remain competitive in the digital landscape. By implementing SEO, you make it easier for potential clients to find, trust, and choose your services.

Understanding the Basics: SEO vs. Traditional Marketing

Traditional marketing for accountants typically includes methods like networking events, referrals, direct mail, print ads, and other offline strategies While these methods still have their place, they often lack the precision and reach of digital marketing, particularly SEO. Here's a comparison to highlight the key differences:

1. Audience Targeting:
   - Traditional Marketing: Relies on broad tactics like ads or mailers, often targeting a wide audience without specificity.
   - SEO: Uses data and analytics to target specific audiences based on search behavior, location, and intent, reaching those most likely to need accounting

services.

2. Cost Efficiency:
   - Traditional Marketing: Can be expensive, with high costs for ad placements, printing, and distribution, often with limited tracking of return on investment.
   - SEO: Offers a more cost-effective approach by targeting users actively searching for your services, leading to higher conversion rates and lower costs per lead.

3. Measurability:
   - Traditional Marketing: Difficult to measure success accurately. For instance, it's hard to track how many people called your office because they saw a print ad.
   - SEO: Provides clear metrics and analytics, allowing you to track every aspect of your campaign, from traffic and rankings to conversions and ROI.

4. Reach:
   - Traditional Marketing: Typically limited by geography and medium. For example, a local newspaper ad will only reach readers of that paper.
   - SEO: Extends your reach to a global or local audience, depending on your goals, with the potential to reach thousands of potential clients searching online.

5. Interaction:
   - Traditional Marketing: Generally a one-way communication with limited interaction, such as reading an ad or receiving a brochure.
   - SEO: Encourages interaction through website visits, form submissions, and content engagement, allowing for a two-way communication channel with potential clients.

6. Adaptability:
   - Traditional Marketing: Changes to campaigns can be slow and costly,

such as reprinting materials or rebooking ads.

   - SEO: Highly adaptable, allowing you to make real-time adjustments to content, keywords, and strategies based on performance data.

7. Longevity:
   - Traditional Marketing: Efforts are often short-lived, such as a one-time ad or event.
   - SEO: Provides long-term benefits, with ongoing optimization efforts continually driving traffic and leads.

By shifting from traditional marketing to SEO, accountants can take advantage of a more efficient, targeted, and measurable approach to attracting new clients. SEO doesn't just replace traditional marketing; it enhances your overall strategy by aligning your services with the evolving ways in which clients search for and choose their accountants.

How This Book Will Help You

This book, "SEO Accounting: For Beginners," is designed to be your comprehensive guide to mastering SEO as an accountant. Whether you're a solo practitioner, part of a small firm, or managing a larger practice, the strategies and insights provided here will empower you to improve your online presence, attract more clients, and grow your business. Here's what you can expect to gain from this book:

1. Step-by-Step Guidance: We break down complex SEO concepts into simple, actionable steps tailored specifically for accountants. From understanding keyword research to optimizing your website, you'll receive clear instructions on how to implement effective SEO strategies.

2. Practical Tools and Tips: Learn about the best tools for keyword research, site optimization, and performance tracking. We'll guide you through how to use these tools effectively to streamline your SEO efforts and achieve better

results.

3. Real-World Examples: Throughout the book, you'll find case studies and examples from other accountants who have successfully used SEO to grow their practices. These real-world insights will help you understand how to apply SEO techniques in your own context.

4. Avoid Common Pitfalls: SEO can be overwhelming, and there are common mistakes that many accountants make when starting out. This book highlights these pitfalls and provides strategies to avoid them, ensuring you stay on the right path.

5. Customized Strategies for Accountants: Unlike general SEO guides, this book focuses on the specific needs of the accounting industry. You'll learn how to create content that resonates with potential clients, optimize for local searches, and leverage your unique expertise to stand out.

6. Ongoing Learning and Improvement: SEO isn't a one-time effort; it's an ongoing process. This book equips you with the knowledge to continue refining and improving your SEO strategy over time, keeping you ahead of the competition.

7. Confidence to Take Control of Your Marketing: One of the biggest benefits of learning SEO is the ability to take control of your marketing efforts. Rather than relying solely on external agencies or costly ad campaigns, you'll have the skills to enhance your own digital presence and make data-driven decisions.

8. Future-Proof Your Practice: As the digital landscape continues to evolve, having a solid understanding of SEO will help you adapt and thrive. This book not only teaches you the fundamentals but also provides insights into emerging trends, ensuring you remain competitive in the years to come.

9. Enhanced Client Relationships: By optimizing your website and content,

you'll create a better user experience for your visitors. This not only attracts new clients but also helps retain existing ones by demonstrating your commitment to accessibility and professionalism.

10. Comprehensive Coverage: Each chapter is carefully crafted to cover all aspects of SEO, from the basics to advanced tactics. Whether you're new to SEO or looking to refine your skills, you'll find valuable information that caters to your level of expertise.

By the end of this book, you will not only understand the importance of SEO for accountants but also have a clear, actionable plan to implement SEO strategies that drive results. You'll be equipped with the tools, knowledge, and confidence needed to enhance your digital presence and grow your accounting practice in today's competitive market.

Getting Started with SEO

SEO, or Search Engine Optimization, is a crucial tool for any accounting practice looking to thrive in the digital age. This chapter will guide you through the essentials of getting started with SEO, covering basic terminology, understanding how search engines work, the importance of SEO specifically for accountants, and setting achievable SEO goals for your practice.

Basic SEO Terminology

Before diving into the intricacies of SEO, it's essential to familiarize yourself with some key terms that you will encounter frequently in this field. Understanding these terms will provide a solid foundation as you start optimizing your accounting practice's online presence.

1. Keywords: Keywords are the words or phrases that people type into search engines when looking for information. In SEO, keywords are crucial because they help search engines understand the content of your website and match it with users' search queries. For accountants, relevant keywords might include "tax preparation services," "small business accounting," or "CPA near me."

2. SERP (Search Engine Results Page): The page displayed by search engines in response to a user's query is known as the SERP. The goal of SEO is to get your website to appear as high as possible on these pages because most users don't look beyond the first page of results.

3. On-Page SEO: This refers to optimization techniques applied directly to your website's content and structure, such as using the right keywords, optimizing title tags and meta descriptions, and ensuring a good user experience.

4. Off-Page SEO: Off-page SEO involves activities that happen outside of your website but still impact your ranking. This includes building back links (links from other websites to yours), social media marketing, and online reputation management.

5. Back links: These are links from other websites that point to your site. Back links are important because they signal to search engines that your content is valuable and trustworthy. The more high-quality back links you have, the better your chances of ranking higher in search results.

6. Meta Tags: Meta tags are snippets of text that describe a page's content; they don't appear on the page itself but in the page's code. The two most important meta tags are the title tag and the meta description. These tags help search engines understand what your page is about and influence whether users click on your link in the SERP.

7. Alt Text: Alt text (alternative text) is used in HTML to describe images. This text helps search engines understand what the images are about, which can also aid in your website's overall SEO.

8. Content Management System (CMS): A CMS is software that helps you create, manage, and modify content on a website without needing specialized technical knowledge. Common CMS platforms include WordPress, Wix, and Square space.

9. Bounce Rate: This is the percentage of visitors who navigate away from your site after viewing only one page. A high bounce rate can indicate that your site's content isn't engaging or relevant to your visitors, which can

negatively impact your SEO.

10. Organic Traffic: This is the traffic that comes to your website from unpaid search results. The primary goal of SEO is to increase organic traffic by improving your website's ranking on SERPs.

11. Analytics: Analytics involves tracking and analyzing data about your website's traffic, such as how many people visit your site, where they come from, and what they do while there. Google Analytics is a popular tool used to gather this data.

Understanding these basic SEO terms will help you navigate the world of SEO more effectively. As you become more familiar with these concepts, you'll be better equipped to optimize your website and attract the right audience.

How Search Engines Work

To successfully implement SEO strategies, it's important to understand how search engines work. Search engines like Google, Bing, and Yahoo are complex systems that use algorithms to index, rank, and display content from the internet. Here's a breakdown of the main processes involved:

1. Crawling: Search engines use automated bots known as crawlers or spiders to scan the internet and find new and updated content. These crawlers follow links from one page to another, collecting data about each page they visit. For example, Google's crawler, Google bot, discovers new content by following links within your site and links from other sites.

2. Indexing: Once the crawlers find your content, it's added to the search engine's index, which is essentially a vast database of information. During indexing, the search engine processes the information it finds on your page, including text, keywords, and images. If your site isn't indexed, it won't appear in search results, making this step crucial.

3. Ranking: After indexing, search engines rank the pages based on relevance to the search query, quality of content, and many other factors. The goal of SEO is to optimize these factors to improve your website's ranking on the SERPs. The higher your site ranks, the more visible it will be to users.

4. Algorithms: Search engines use complex algorithms to determine how to rank pages. These algorithms consider hundreds of factors, including keyword usage, site structure, back links, mobile-friendliness, and user experience. Google, for example, constantly updates its algorithm to provide the best possible results for users, which is why SEO is an ongoing process.

5. Relevance and Authority: Search engines strive to provide the most relevant and authoritative results for any given query. Relevance is determined by how well your content matches the search intent of the query, while authority is often measured by the quality and quantity of back links pointing to your site.

6. User Signals: Search engines also take into account user signals such as click-through rate (CTR), bounce rate, and time on page. These signals help search engines gauge the quality and relevance of your content based on user interactions.

Understanding these processes can help you optimize your accounting website effectively. By ensuring your site is crawlable, indexable, and optimized for the factors that algorithms prioritize, you can improve your chances of ranking higher on search engines and attracting more clients.

The Importance of SEO for Accountants

SEO is crucial for accountants for several reasons, particularly in an era where clients increasingly rely on online searches to find and evaluate professional services. Here's why SEO should be a key component of your marketing strategy:

1. Increased Visibility and Traffic: The primary benefit of SEO is increased visibility in search engines, which directly translates to more traffic. For accountants, this means more potential clients discovering your services when they search for relevant terms like "tax accountant near me" or "small business bookkeeping services."

2. Credibility and Trust: Websites that appear at the top of search results are perceived as more credible and trustworthy. A strong SEO strategy not only helps you climb the ranks but also builds a professional image, giving potential clients confidence in your expertise.

3. Cost-Effective Marketing: Compared to traditional advertising methods like print ads or direct mail, SEO is more cost-effective. While SEO requires an initial investment of time and resources, it delivers sustainable, long-term results by continuously driving organic traffic to your website without ongoing costs.

4. Targeted Audience Reach: SEO allows you to target specific audiences based on keywords that are relevant to your services. This means you're attracting visitors who are actively searching for the accounting services you provide, increasing the likelihood of conversions.

5. Local SEO for Accountants: Local SEO is particularly important for accountants who serve specific geographical areas. By optimizing for local search terms and ensuring your Google My Business profile is up to date, you can attract clients from your immediate area, making it easier for them to choose your services.

6. Adaptation to Changing Consumer Behavior: The way people search for services has changed significantly with the rise of digital technology. Potential clients now expect to find accountants online quickly and easily. By optimizing your website for search engines, you meet these expectations and position your practice as accessible and client-focused.

7. Competitive Advantage: Many accounting firms have not yet fully embraced SEO, providing an opportunity for those who do. By optimizing your website, you can get ahead of competitors who rely solely on traditional marketing tactics, capturing market share that might otherwise be lost.

8. Enhanced User Experience: SEO isn't just about search engines; it's also about improving the user experience. Good SEO practices involve optimizing site speed, ensuring mobile compatibility, and creating content that is relevant and engaging. This results in a better overall experience for your visitors, encouraging them to stay longer and explore more of your services.

9. Long-Term Growth: SEO is not a one-time effort; it's an ongoing process that can deliver long-term growth. As you continue to optimize your website and content, you'll see sustained improvements in your search rankings, traffic, and client acquisition.

10. Data-Driven Insights: SEO provides valuable data and insights into your audience's behavior, preferences, and search habits. By analyzing this data, you can make informed decisions about your marketing strategy, refine your services, and better meet your clients' needs.

In summary, SEO is not just an option but a necessity for accountants who want to remain competitive and grow their practices in today's digital landscape. By investing in SEO, you can ensure that your services are visible, credible, and accessible to the clients who need them most.

Setting SEO Goals for Your Accounting Practice

To achieve success with SEO, it's important to set clear, achievable goals that align with your business objectives. Setting the right SEO goals will help you focus your efforts and measure your progress effectively. Here are some steps to guide you in setting SEO goals for your accounting practice:

1. Define Your Objectives: Start by identifying what you want to achieve with SEO. Common objectives for accountants include increasing website traffic, generating more leads, improving online visibility, and building brand credibility. Your objectives should align with your overall business goals such as growing your client base, expanding into new markets, or establishing your firm as an authority in specific accounting services.

2. Set Specific, Measurable Goals: Once you've defined your objectives, translate them into specific, measurable goals. For example, instead of a vague goal like "increase website traffic," aim for something concrete like "increase organic traffic by 30% in the next six months." Measurable goals help you track progress and make adjustments as needed.

3. Identify Key Performance Indicators (KPIs): KPIs are metrics that help you measure the success of your SEO efforts. Common SEO KPIs include:
   - Organic Traffic: The number of visitors coming to your site from unpaid search results.
   - Keyword Rankings: The position of your targeted keywords on SERPs.
   - Click-Through Rate (CTR): The percentage of users who click on your site link after seeing it in search results.
   - Bounce Rate: The percentage of visitors who leave your site after viewing only one page.
   - Conversion Rate: The percentage of visitors who take a desired action, such as filling out a contact form or signing up for a newsletter.

4. Set Realistic Timeframes: It's important to set realistic time frames for achieving your SEO goals. SEO is a long-term strategy, and significant improvements can take months to materialize. For instance, achieving a first-page ranking for a competitive keyword might take six months to a year, depending on the level of competition and your current standing.

5. Prioritize Your Efforts: Not all SEO activities will have the same impact, so it's crucial to prioritize your efforts based on potential ROI. For example,

if local SEO is a key part of your strategy, prioritize optimizing your Google My Business profile and acquiring local back links. Similarly, if your website is already getting traffic but not converting, focus on improving on-page SEO and the user experience.

6. Create an Action Plan: Develop a detailed action plan outlining the specific steps you will take to achieve your goals. This might include conducting keyword research, creating new content, optimizing existing pages, building back links, or setting up analytics to track your progress. Your action plan should be organized, with tasks assigned clear deadlines and responsible parties if you're working with a team.

7. Monitor and Adjust: SEO is dynamic, with search engine algorithms and user behaviors constantly evolving. Regularly monitor your performance against your KPIs and be prepared to adjust your strategy as needed. If a particular keyword isn't performing as expected, consider tweaking your content or exploring alternative keywords. Continuous improvement is key to long-term success in SEO.

8. Celebrate Milestones: Recognizing and celebrating small wins along the way is important for maintaining motivation and momentum. Whether it's moving up a few spots in rankings for a key term or hitting a new high in website traffic, acknowledging these milestones can help keep your SEO efforts on track.

9. Focus on Value Creation: At the core of successful SEO is the creation of value for your audience. Always ensure that your SEO efforts align with providing useful, relevant, and high-quality content that meets the needs of your potential clients. This approach not only improves your SEO metrics but also strengthens client relationships and builds trust in your accounting practice.

10. Align SEO Goals with Business Goals: Ultimately, your SEO goals should

support your broader business objectives. Regularly review how your SEO efforts contribute to achieving these larger goals and make adjustments as necessary. For instance, if your business goal is to increase revenue from small business clients, ensure that your SEO strategy includes targeting keywords and content that resonate with that audience.

By setting clear, achievable SEO goals and aligning them with your overall business objectives, you can create a focused and effective SEO strategy that drives tangible results for your accounting practice. SEO is not a set-and-forget solution; it requires ongoing effort, monitoring, and refinement. However, the rewards in terms of increased visibility, credibility, and client acquisition make it a worthwhile investment for any accountant looking to grow their business in the digital age.

Getting started with SEO can feel overwhelming, but breaking it down into manageable steps makes it much more approachable. By understanding basic SEO terminology, grasping how search engines work, recognizing the importance of SEO for your accounting practice, and setting clear, actionable goals, you lay the groundwork for a successful SEO strategy. As you move forward, remember that SEO is an ongoing journey of learning, adapting, and optimizing. With commitment and the right approach, you can harness the power of SEO to attract more clients, enhance your digital presence, and achieve sustained growth for your accounting practice.

Keyword Research for Accountants

Keyword research is one of the most critical aspects of SEO and serves as the foundation for your online marketing efforts. For accountants, effective keyword research helps you understand the language your potential clients use when searching for accounting services online, allowing you to optimize your website and content to attract the right audience. This chapter will cover the essentials of keyword research, including understanding keywords and their importance, the best tools for conducting keyword research, how to identify high-value keywords in accounting, and the strategic use of long-tail keywords.

Understanding Keywords and Their Importance

Keywords are the terms and phrases that users type into search engines when looking for information, services, or products. In the context of SEO, keywords are the bridge that connects searchers to your website. For accountants, keywords represent the specific services, expertise, and solutions that your potential clients are searching for online.

Why Are Keywords Important?

1. Visibility and Ranking: Keywords play a crucial role in determining how your website ranks on search engine results pages (SERPs). When your content is optimized for relevant keywords, it has a better chance of appearing in front of users searching for those terms, increasing your website's visibility.

2. Targeting the Right Audience: Using the correct keywords ensures that your content reaches the most relevant audience. For accountants, this means attracting potential clients who are actively seeking your services, whether it's tax preparation, auditing, or financial consulting.

3. Understanding Search Intent: Keywords help you understand the intent behind a user's search. By analyzing keywords, you can gauge whether a searcher is looking for general information, comparing service providers, or ready to hire an accountant. This understanding allows you to create content that matches the user's intent, guiding them through the client journey.

4. Competitive Advantage: Effective keyword research helps you identify opportunities where you can outperform competitors. By targeting less competitive keywords or niches that are undeserved, you can carve out a space in the market where your firm can stand out.

5. Content Planning and Strategy: Keywords are the foundation of your content strategy. They inform the topics you should cover, the questions you should answer, and the services you should highlight. This strategic approach ensures that your content is not only relevant but also highly targeted to your audience's needs.

6. Measuring Success: Keywords also serve as benchmarks for measuring the success of your SEO efforts. By tracking how your targeted keywords are performing in terms of ranking and traffic, you can assess the effectiveness of your strategies and make data-driven adjustments.

In summary, keywords are essential because they guide both search engines and users to your content. For accountants, selecting the right keywords is the first step toward building a strong online presence that attracts and converts potential clients.

Tools for Effective Keyword Research

Conducting effective keyword research requires the use of specialized tools that can help you identify, analyze, and select the best keywords for your accounting practice. Here are some of the most popular and effective keyword research tools that accountants can use:

1. Google Keyword Planner: Google's Keyword Planner is a free tool that provides insights into keyword search volumes, competition levels, and keyword suggestions. It's a great starting point for identifying which keywords are popular within your industry. You can input your own keywords or phrases related to accounting and get a list of related keywords along with their average monthly searches and competition data.

2. Ahrefs: Ahrefs is a comprehensive SEO tool that offers in-depth keyword research capabilities. It provides keyword difficulty scores, search volume data, and click-through rates (CTR) for keywords, making it easier to assess which keywords are worth targeting. Ahrefs also allows you to analyze your competitors' keywords, uncovering opportunities to outrank them.

3. SEMrush: SEMrush is another powerful SEO tool that offers extensive keyword research features. It provides keyword suggestions, search trends, and keyword difficulty scores. SEMrush also has a unique feature called the Keyword Magic Tool, which allows you to explore keyword variations and related terms, helping you expand your keyword list.

4. Moz Keyword Explorer: Moz Keyword Explorer is a user-friendly tool that offers keyword suggestions, search volume, and difficulty scores. It also provides insights into organic click-through rates and prioritizes keywords based on their potential impact. Moz's tool is particularly useful for identifying long-tail keywords that can drive highly targeted traffic to your site.

5. Ubersuggest: Ubersuggest, developed by Neil Patel, is a free keyword research tool that offers keyword suggestions, search volume data, and

keyword difficulty scores. It's especially helpful for beginners who are looking for an easy-to-use tool without a steep learning curve. Ubersuggest also provides content ideas based on your keywords, aiding in content planning.

6. Keyword Surfer: Keyword Surfer is a browser extension that integrates directly with Google's search engine results pages, providing keyword data such as search volume and related keywords alongside your search results. This tool is particularly useful for conducting quick keyword research on the go.

7. AnswerThePublic: AnswerThePublic is a unique tool that visualizes keyword data by showing you questions and phrases that people commonly search for in relation to a keyword. For accountants, this can be valuable for identifying content ideas that address specific questions or concerns that potential clients may have.

8. Google Trends: Google Trends allows you to analyze the popularity of search terms over time. It's useful for identifying seasonal trends in keyword searches, which can be particularly relevant for accounting services that have peak periods, such as tax season.

Using these tools, you can gather a wide array of keyword data, analyze the competition, and make informed decisions about which keywords to target in your SEO strategy. Each tool offers unique features, so using a combination of them can provide a more comprehensive view of the keyword landscape.

Identifying High-Value Keywords in Accounting

Identifying high-value keywords is critical to ensuring that your SEO efforts drive meaningful results. High-value keywords are those that not only have a reasonable search volume but also align closely with your services and the needs of your target audience. Here's how you can identify high-value keywords for your accounting practice:

KEYWORD RESEARCH FOR ACCOUNTANTS

1. Start with Seed Keywords: Seed keywords are the core terms that directly relate to your services. For accountants, these might include words like "accounting," "bookkeeping," "tax preparation," and "CPA." Use these seed keywords as the starting point for your research, entering them into keyword research tools to find related terms.

2. Consider Search Intent: Not all keywords are created equal. To identify high-value keywords, you need to consider the search intent behind them. Are users looking for information, comparing services, or ready to hire an accountant? High-value keywords typically have commercial or transactional intent, meaning the searcher is close to making a purchasing decision. Keywords like "hire an accountant for small business" or "best tax accountant near me" indicate a strong intent to take action.

3. Evaluate Keyword Difficulty: Keyword difficulty is a measure of how hard it will be to rank for a particular keyword. High-value keywords often have moderate difficulty, balancing search volume and competition. If a keyword is too competitive, it may be hard to achieve a top ranking, especially for newer or smaller accounting practices. Focus on keywords that have a realistic ranking potential given your current SEO standing.

4. Analyze Search Volume and Trends: High-value keywords should have a decent search volume, indicating that people are actively searching for those terms. However, volume isn't everything. Look for keywords with consistent or growing search trends, which suggest sustained interest. Seasonal keywords, like those related to tax preparation, can also be valuable at certain times of the year.

5. Use Competitor Analysis: Analyze the keywords that your competitors are ranking for to identify potential opportunities. Tools like Ahrefs and SEMrush allow you to see which keywords are driving traffic to your competitors' sites. If you notice that a competitor is ranking well for a keyword that you haven't targeted, it may be worth adding it to your list.

6. Focus on Specific Services: Accountants often offer a wide range of services, from personal tax preparation to corporate auditing. Identify keywords that are specific to the services you most want to promote. For example, "small business bookkeeping services" or "IRS audit assistance" are more specific and targeted than broad terms like "accountant."

7. Incorporate Local Keywords: For accountants, local SEO is often crucial. Incorporating location-based keywords, such as "accountant in [city]" or "tax services near me," can help you connect with clients in your area. Local keywords typically have lower competition and are highly valuable for attracting geographically relevant traffic.

8. Refine with Long-Tail Keywords: Long-tail keywords, which are more detailed and specific phrases, often have lower search volumes but higher conversion rates. For example, "affordable tax accountant for freelancers" is a long-tail keyword that, while more niche, indicates a highly specific need and intent.

Identifying high-value keywords is about finding the right balance between search volume, competition, and relevance to your services. By focusing on these factors, you can build a targeted keyword strategy that drives quality traffic and generates leads for your accounting practice.

Long-Tail Keywords: Your Secret Weapon

Long-tail keywords are longer, more specific phrases that typically have lower search volumes than broader keywords but offer numerous advantages, particularly for niche markets like accounting. These keywords are often less competitive and can attract highly targeted traffic that is more likely to convert into clients.

Why Long-Tail Keywords Matter

1. Higher Conversion Rates: Long-tail keywords often reflect more specific search intent meaning users who search for these terms are further along in the decision-making process. For instance, someone searching for "best small business accountant in New York" is likely closer to hiring an accountant than someone searching for the broader term "accountant."

2.Lower Competition: Long-tail keywords generally have less competition than broad keywords, making it easier for your accounting practice to rank higher on search engine results pages. This is especially beneficial for smaller firms or those just starting with SEO, as it allows you to gain visibility without having to compete with larger, more established firms targeting broader terms.

3. Improved Relevance: By using long-tail keywords, you can tailor your content more precisely to the needs and concerns of your target audience. This improves the relevance of your site's content, which not only helps with search engine rankings but also enhances the user experience, making visitors more likely to engage with your site and contact you for services.

4. Better User Experience: Content that is optimized for long-tail keywords tends to be more specific and detailed, providing users with exactly the information they're looking for. This can reduce bounce rates and keep visitors on your site longer, signaling to search engines that your site is valuable and worth ranking higher.

5. Voice Search Optimization: With the rise of voice search through devices like smartphones and smart speakers, users are increasingly using conversational, question-based queries. Long-tail keywords often align closely with how people speak and ask questions, making them highly effective for capturing voice search traffic. For example, a query like "who is the best accountant for small businesses near me" is a natural fit for long-tail keyword optimization.

6. Flexibility and Adaptability: Long-tail keywords offer the flexibility to target niche areas and adapt your content strategy over time. As search trends change or as your accounting practice evolves, you can adjust your long-tail keyword strategy to match new services or emerging client needs without overhauling your entire SEO approach.

How to Identify and Use Long-Tail Keywords

1. Start with Seed Keywords: Begin by using your main seed keywords as the basis for finding related long-tail keywords. Input these into keyword research tools like Ahrefs, SEMrush, or Google Keyword Planner to generate lists of longer, more specific keywords that include your core terms.

2. Explore Question-Based Keywords: Tools like AnswerThePublic and Keywords Everywhere can help you find question-based keywords, which often reflect user intent more clearly. For example, instead of targeting "tax preparation," consider questions like "how to prepare taxes for a small business" or "what documents are needed for tax preparation."

3. Leverage Google's Auto complete and Related Searches: Google's search bar can be a valuable source of long-tail keywords. As you type in a broad keyword, Google Auto complete will suggest related searches that are popular among users. At the bottom of the search results page, Google also lists related searches, which can provide additional long-tail keyword ideas.

4. Use Competitor Analysis: Look at your competitors' websites to see which long-tail keywords they are targeting. Tools like Ahrefs or SEMrush allow you to analyze competitor content and identify long-tail keywords that drive traffic to their sites, giving you insights into what might work for your own strategy.

5. Incorporate Long-Tail Keywords into Content: Once you've identified your long-tail keywords, incorporate them naturally into your content. This

includes blog posts, service pages, FAQs, and other relevant sections of your website. Ensure that the content addresses the specific needs or questions implied by the keywords, providing valuable and actionable information to your audience.

6. Optimize for Local and Niche Services: If your accounting practice offers specialized services or caters to a specific location, incorporate these details into your long-tail keywords. For example, instead of just "tax services," consider "tax services for independent contractors in Los Angeles." This approach narrows your focus, increasing the likelihood of attracting clients who are searching for exactly what you offer.

7. Monitor Performance and Adjust: As with any SEO strategy, it's important to monitor the performance of your long-tail keywords. Use tools like Google Analytics and Google Search Console to track which keywords are driving traffic and conversions. If certain long-tail keywords aren't performing as expected, refine your content or try different variations to see what resonates better with your audience.

8. Create Targeted Content Hubs: Organize your content around key themes or services using long-tail keywords to create content hubs. For example, if you specialize in accounting for small businesses, develop a series of articles, guides, and FAQs centered on various aspects of small business accounting all optimized with relevant long-tail keywords. This approach helps build authority in your niche and improves your chances of ranking for multiple related searches.

Examples of Long-Tail Keywords for Accountants

- "Best tax accountant for freelancers in [city]"
  - "Affordable bookkeeping services for startups"
  - "How to choose an accountant for small businesses"
  - "CPA for non-profits near me"

- "Financial planning services for retirees in [city]"
- "Virtual accounting services for e-commerce businesses"
- "Estate tax preparation for high-net-worth individuals"

These examples illustrate how long-tail keywords can target specific needs, services, or audiences, making it easier for potential clients to find your accounting practice when searching for highly relevant terms.

Conclusion

Keyword research is a foundational element of any successful SEO strategy, especially for accountants looking to attract the right clients. By understanding the importance of keywords, leveraging effective research tools, identifying high-value terms, and strategically using long-tail keywords, you can optimize your online presence to reach your target audience more effectively.

As you continue to refine your keyword strategy, remember that SEO is an ongoing process that requires regular monitoring, analysis, and adaptation. The digital landscape and search behavior of users are constantly evolving, and staying attuned to these changes will help you maintain a competitive edge. By focusing on providing valuable, relevant, and targeted content through well-researched keywords, your accounting practice can achieve sustained growth and success in the digital marketplace.

On-Page SEO Essentials

On-page SEO involves optimizing various elements on your website to improve its visibility and ranking on search engines like Google. It focuses on both the content you provide and the technical aspects of your site. By mastering on-page SEO, you can ensure that your website is easily understood by search engines and provides a great experience for visitors. This chapter will guide you through the essentials of on-page SEO, including optimizing your website structure, crafting SEO-friendly content, using meta tags, titles, and descriptions, and understanding the role of headers and alt text.

Optimizing Your Website Structure

A well-organized website structure is crucial for both users and search engines. It helps visitors navigate your site easily and allows search engines to crawl and index your pages effectively. Here are some key steps to optimize your website structure:

1. Create a Clear Hierarchy: Your website should have a clear and logical hierarchy. This means having a main menu with your primary categories and submenus for related subcategories. For example, an accounting website might have main categories like "Services," "About Us," "Resources," and "Contact Us," with subcategories under "Services" for "Tax Preparation," "Bookkeeping," and "Financial Consulting."

2. Use a Simple URL Structure: URLs should be easy to read and include relevant keywords. Instead of complex URLs with random letters and numbers, use descriptive words that tell users what the page is about. For example, use "www.youraccountingsite.com/tax-preparation" instead of "www.youraccountingsite.com/page123."

3. Implement Internal Linking: Internal linking involves linking from one page of your website to another. This not only helps users find related content easily but also helps search engines understand the relationship between pages on your site. For instance, if you have a blog post about "tax preparation tips," you can link it to your "Tax Preparation Services" page.

4. Optimize for Mobile Devices: Many users will visit your site from mobile devices, so it's crucial that your website is mobile-friendly. Use a responsive design that adjusts to different screen sizes and ensures that buttons and links are easy to click on mobile devices.

5. Improve Site Speed: A slow-loading website can frustrate visitors and cause them to leave, which can negatively impact your SEO. Use tools like Google Page Speed Insights to check your site's speed and get recommendations on how to improve it. Common fixes include optimizing images, reducing server response times, and minimizing the use of heavy scripts.

6. Use Breadcrumbs: Breadcrumbs are small navigation aids that show users where they are on your website and how to return to previous pages. They also help search engines understand your site's structure. For example, on a "Tax Preparation" page, a breadcrumb might look like this: "Home > Services > Tax Preparation."

7. Submit a Sitemap: A sitemap is a file that lists all the pages on your website. Submitting a sitemap to search engines like Google helps them crawl your site more effectively. Most website platforms, like WordPress, offer plugins that can automatically generate and update your sitemap.

By optimizing your website structure, you create a better experience for your users and make it easier for search engines to find and rank your content. A well-structured site is the foundation of good on-page SEO and sets the stage for the rest of your optimization efforts.

Crafting SEO-Friendly Content

Content is at the heart of SEO. Crafting SEO-friendly content means creating material that is valuable to your audience and optimized for search engines. Here are the key steps to creating content that ranks well:

1. Focus on High-Quality, Relevant Content: Your content should address the needs and interests of your target audience. For accountants, this could include blog posts about tax tips, guides on financial planning, or explanations of complex accounting concepts. Always aim to provide value—content that answers questions, solves problems, or offers useful insights.

2. Incorporate Keywords Naturally: Use your target keywords in your content, but do so naturally. Keywords should fit within the context of your writing and should not feel forced. Include them in key places like the first paragraph, headings, and throughout the text, but avoid keyword stuffing, which can make your content feel unnatural and can harm your SEO.

3. Write Clear and Concise Content: Search engines favor content that is easy to read and understand. Use short paragraphs, bullet points, and subheadings to break up the text. This makes it easier for users to skim and find the information they need. Avoid using complex jargon unless it's essential, and always define any technical terms.

4. Use Internal and External Links: Linking to other relevant pages on your site (internal links) helps guide users to additional content and keeps them engaged longer. External links to authoritative sources can also add value to your content and enhance its credibility. For example, linking to official

tax resources or recognized financial organizations can provide additional context and depth.

5. Update Content Regularly: Fresh content is more appealing to both users and search engines. Regularly update your existing content to ensure it remains relevant and accurate. For example, if you have a blog post on tax laws, update it yearly to reflect the latest changes.

6. Include a Call to Action (CTA): Every piece of content should have a purpose, whether it's to inform, educate, or persuade. Including a CTA encourages users to take the next step, such as contacting you for a consultation, downloading a resource, or subscribing to your newsletter.

7. Optimize for Featured Snippets: Featured snippets are short, direct answers that appear at the top of Google's search results. They are highly valuable for visibility. To optimize for featured snippets, structure your content in a way that directly answers common questions, using bullet points, numbered lists, or concise paragraphs.

8. Ensure Readability: Use a simple and clear writing style that matches the reading level of your audience. Tools like the Hemingway App can help you assess and improve the readability of your content, making it more accessible and engaging for a wider audience.

Crafting SEO-friendly content is about balancing user needs with search engine optimization techniques. By providing valuable information in an accessible format and strategically using keywords, links, and CTAs, you can create content that not only ranks well but also resonates with your audience.

Using Meta Tags, Titles, and Descriptions

Meta tags, titles, and descriptions are essential components of on-page SEO that help search engines understand your content and encourage users to click on your links in search results. Here's how to optimize them effectively:

1. Title Tags: The title tag is one of the most important on-page SEO elements. It appears as the clickable headline in search results and should be clear, concise, and include your primary keyword. Keep your title tags under 60 characters to ensure they display properly on all devices. For example, a good title tag for an accounting service might be "Tax Preparation Services for Small Businesses | [Your Company Name]."

2. Meta Descriptions: The meta description is a short summary that appears under the title tag in search results. It should provide a compelling reason for users to click on your link. While meta descriptions don't directly affect rankings, they do influence click-through rates, which can impact your SEO. Include your primary keyword and keep the description under 160 characters. For example, "Expert tax preparation services for small businesses. Get accurate, timely help from our certified accountants."

3. Meta Keywords: Although meta keywords were once a staple of SEO, they are no longer a significant factor in search engine rankings. Most modern SEO strategies do not include meta keywords, as they are often ignored by major search engines like Google. Focus on title tags and meta descriptions instead.

4. Use Unique Tags for Each Page: Every page on your site should have its own unique title tag and meta description that accurately reflect the content on that page. Avoid duplicating tags across multiple pages, as this can confuse search engines and dilute your SEO efforts.

5. Optimize for Click-Through Rate (CTR): To improve your CTR, write engaging titles and descriptions that stand out in search results. Use action words, address the user directly, and highlight the benefits of clicking on your link. For example, instead of a generic title like "Accounting Services," try "Save Money with Expert Accounting Services in [City]."

6. Include Calls to Action in Descriptions: A well-crafted meta description can include a call to action, encouraging users to take the next step. For example, "Need help with your taxes? Contact our team of experts today for a free consultation."

Meta tags, titles, and descriptions are small elements that pack a big punch in terms of SEO. By crafting them carefully and incorporating relevant keywords, you can significantly improve the visibility and attractiveness of your site in search results.

The Role of Headers and Alt Text in SEO

Headers (H1, H2, H3, etc.) and alt text are additional on-page elements that play important roles in structuring your content and making it accessible to search engines and users alike. Here's how to use them effectively:

1. Headers (H1, H2, H3, etc.): Headers are used to organize your content into sections and subsections. The H1 tag is typically used for the main title of the page, while H2, H3, and other header tags are used for subheadings. Headers help search engines understand the structure and main topics of your content, and they make your content easier for users to read.

- Use Only One H1 Tag: The H1 tag should be used only once per page and should include your main keyword. It should accurately describe the page's content, such as "Comprehensive Tax Preparation Services."

- Use H2 and H3
   3 Tags for Subsections: Use H2 tags for main sections of your content and H3 tags for subsections under those. This hierarchy helps break up your content and makes it more readable. For example, an H2 might be "Our Tax Preparation Services," with H3 tags for "Individual Tax Preparation" and "Business Tax Preparation."

- Include Keywords in Headers: While it's important not to overuse keywords, incorporating them naturally into your headers can help search engines understand what your content is about. For instance, if your target keyword is "small business bookkeeping," a relevant H2 might be "Bookkeeping Services for Small Businesses."

- Improve User Experience: Headers aren't just for SEO; they also enhance the user experience by making your content more skimmable. Many users don't read entire pages—they scan for the information they need. Clear and descriptive headers guide them through your content efficiently.

2. Alt Text for Images: Alt text (alternative text) is used to describe images on your website. It serves two main purposes: providing a text alternative for visually impaired users and helping search engines understand the content of your images.

- Describe the Image Clearly: Alt text should be a clear and concise description of what the image shows. For example, if you have a photo of your team, a good alt text might be "Accounting team at [Your Company Name] office in [City]."

- Include Keywords Where Relevant: If appropriate, include keywords in your alt text, but only if they naturally fit the description. For instance, for an image of a tax form, alt text could be "Completed tax form for small business accounting."

- Avoid Keyword Stuffing: Alt text should make sense to human readers. Avoid stuffing it with keywords, as this can lead to a poor user experience and potential penalties from search engines.

- Enhance Accessibility: Including descriptive alt text helps make your site accessible to users with disabilities who rely on screen readers. This not only improves the user experience but also reflects well on your brand as inclusive and user-friendly.

3. Image File Names and Sizes: Before uploading images to your site, make sure their file names are descriptive and include relevant keywords. Instead of a generic file name like "IMG1234.jpg," use a name like "small-business-tax-form.jpg." Also, optimize image file sizes to improve your site's loading speed, as large images can slow down your website and negatively impact SEO.

4. Structured Data and Schema Markup: While not directly related to headers or alt text, using structured data or schema markup can further enhance how search engines interpret your content. Structured data provides additional context to search engines, allowing them to display rich snippets (like star ratings or product prices) in search results. This can improve your site's visibility and click-through rate.

On-page SEO is an essential part of building a strong online presence for your accounting practice. By optimizing your website structure, crafting SEO-friendly content, using meta tags, titles, and descriptions effectively, and understanding the role of headers and alt text, you can significantly improve your website's search engine rankings and user experience.

These elements work together to ensure that your content is accessible, relevant, and easy to navigate for both users and search engines. On-page SEO is not a one-time task but an ongoing process that requires regular updates and adjustments as you create new content and refine your existing material.

By mastering these on-page SEO essentials, you set a solid foundation for your overall SEO strategy, helping your accounting practice attract more visitors, convert them into clients, and ultimately grow your business in the competitive digital landscape. Remember, SEO is a long-term investment that pays off with consistent effort and attention to detail. As you continue to optimize your site, keep your audience's needs at the forefront, and your SEO success will follow.

A well-executed content strategy is crucial for accountants who want to enhance their online presence, attract potential clients, and establish authority in their field. Content is the backbone of digital marketing, and when done right, it serves as a powerful tool for building trust and credibility with your audience. In this chapter, we will explore the key components of developing an effective content strategy for accountants, including creating a content plan, understanding the best types of content, focusing on value-driven material, and leveraging case studies and testimonials.

Developing a Content Plan

A content plan serves as a road map for your content creation and distribution efforts. It outlines what types of content you will produce, when and how often you will publish, and how you will promote it to your target audience. Developing a content plan ensures consistency, helps you stay organized, and allows you to strategically align your content with your business goals.

1. Define Your Goals: Start by identifying the primary goals of your content strategy. Common objectives for accountants include generating leads, educating potential clients, building brand awareness, and establishing authority in the accounting field. Be specific about what you want to achieve. For example, you might set a goal to increase website traffic by 30% over the next six months or to generate 50 new leads per month through content marketing.

2. Understand Your Audience: Knowing your audience is key to creating content that resonates with them. Develop buyer personas to represent your ideal clients. Consider factors such as their business size, industry, financial challenges, and the accounting services they need. For instance, if your target

audience consists of small business owners, your content should address topics like cash flow management, tax planning, and bookkeeping.

3. Conduct a Content Audit: If you already have existing content, perform a content audit to evaluate what's working and what isn't. Identify content gaps and opportunities for improvement. Look at metrics such as page views, time on page, and conversion rates to determine which topics and formats are most effective in engaging your audience.

4. Set a Content Calendar: A content calendar is a schedule that outlines when and where you will publish content. It helps you plan ahead, stay consistent, and ensure that you're covering a variety of topics relevant to your audience. Your calendar should include details such as content types (blog posts, articles, videos), publication dates, target keywords, and promotional strategies.

5. Choose Your Content Formats: Accountants can benefit from various content formats, including blog posts, articles, guides, info graphics, videos, webinars, and podcasts. The key is to select formats that align with your audience's preferences and the resources you have available. For example, blog posts and articles are great for in-depth analysis, while info graphics can simplify complex financial information.

6. Align Content with the Buyer's Journey: Different types of content serve different purposes at various stages of the buyer's journey. For example, blog posts and social media content are ideal for the awareness stage, helping potential clients discover your services. Detailed guides and webinars work well in the consideration stage, providing deeper insights and building trust. Finally, case studies and testimonials are effective in the decision stage, demonstrating your expertise and the results you can achieve.

7. Measure and Adjust: Regularly review the performance of your content to see how well it's meeting your goals. Use analytics tools like Google Analytics to track metrics such as traffic, engagement, and conversions. Based on this

data, adjust your content plan as needed. For instance, if blog posts about tax tips are driving the most traffic, consider expanding on that topic with more posts or a detailed guide.

Developing a content plan requires careful planning and ongoing adjustments, but it provides the structure needed to create consistent, high-quality content that supports your business objectives.

Blog Posts, Articles, and Guides: What Works Best

Choosing the right types of content is crucial for engaging your audience and achieving your goals. While there are many content formats to consider, blog posts, articles, and guides are particularly effective for accountants. Here's a closer look at what works best and why:

1. Blog Posts: Blog posts are one of the most versatile and accessible types of content. They allow you to cover a wide range of topics, from timely tax updates to tips on managing business finances. Blog posts are typically shorter (around 600–1,200 words) and are ideal for addressing specific questions or concerns your audience may have. They are easy to share on social media, can be optimized for SEO, and help drive regular traffic to your website.

- Tips for Success: Use clear and engaging headlines, incorporate relevant keywords, and break up the text with subheadings, bullet points, and images. Aim to publish new posts regularly to keep your blog fresh and relevant.

2. Articles: Articles are similar to blog posts but are often more in-depth and formal. They can be used to explore complex accounting topics or provide detailed analysis on industry trends. Articles are a great way to demonstrate your expertise and can be published on your website, in industry publications, or on third-party platforms like LinkedIn.

- Tips for Success: Focus on delivering high-quality, well-researched content.

Use credible sources, include data and statistics to support your points, and aim for a professional tone that reflects your brand's authority in the field.

3. Guides: Guides are longer pieces of content that provide comprehensive coverage of a particular topic. For example, an accounting guide might cover everything a small business owner needs to know about preparing for tax season. Guides are valuable because they offer a deep dive into subjects that matter to your audience, positioning your firm as a trusted resource.

- Tips for Success: Structure your guides clearly, using sections and subheadings to make them easy to navigate. Include practical tips, checklists, or templates that readers can use. Consider offering guides as downloadable PDFs to capture leads by requiring users to provide their email addresses.

4. What Works Best?: The best type of content depends on your audience's needs and your business goals. Blog posts are great for keeping your audience engaged with regular updates, while articles and guides offer more detailed insights and establish your expertise. A balanced mix of these formats can help you reach a wider audience and cater to different preferences.

5. Re purposing Content: Don't be afraid to repurposed content across different formats. A blog post can be expanded into a full article, or key points from a guide can be turned into a series of blog posts. Re purposing not only saves time but also maximizes the value of your content by reaching different audience segments.

By focusing on blog posts, articles, and guides, you can create a diverse content strategy that engages your audience, answers their questions, and showcases your expertise.

Creating Value-Driven Content for Your Audience

The core of any successful content strategy is creating value-driven content that addresses the specific needs and interests of your audience. For accountants, this means offering content that not only informs but also provides practical solutions and insights that help your clients succeed.

1. Identify Pain Points: To create value-driven content, start by identifying the common pain points and challenges your audience faces. For small business owners, this might include cash flow management, understanding tax obligations, or keeping up with regulatory changes. For individuals, it could involve personal budgeting, tax planning, or retirement savings.

2. Offer Practical Solutions: Value-driven content goes beyond just providing information; it offers actionable solutions that your audience can apply. For example, a blog post on "5 Tips to Reduce Your Business Tax Bill" not only educates but also gives readers practical steps they can take. Guides on "How to Prepare for an IRS Audit" or "A Step-by-Step Guide to Setting Up Your Accounting Software" provide hands-on assistance that readers can follow.

3. Be Educational, Not Promotional: While it's important to promote your services, content that is overly sales-focused can turn readers away. Instead, focus on educating your audience. By providing valuable insights and demonstrating your expertise, you build trust and make your audience more likely to consider your services when they need them.

4. Use Real-World Examples: Incorporate real-world examples or case studies that illustrate the points you're making. This not only makes your content more relatable but also shows that you have experience solving similar problems for other clients. For example, if you're writing about cash flow management, include a brief case study of how you helped a client improve their cash flow through specific strategies.

5. Keep It Accessible: Accounting can be a complex and intimidating subject for many people. Your content should aim to demystify these topics, using clear language and avoiding unnecessary jargon. Include definitions of key

terms, use visuals like charts or info graphics to simplify data, and provide examples that make the content easier to understand.

6. Engage with Your Audience: Encourage engagement by asking questions, inviting feedback, or prompting readers to share their experiences. For example, you might end a blog post with, "What's your biggest challenge when it comes to tax preparation? Let us know in the comments!" Engaging with your audience not only builds community but also provides insights into what content will be most valuable to them.

7. Provide Timely and Relevant Content: Stay current with industry news, regulatory changes, and seasonal topics relevant to your audience. For instance, provide content about tax preparation tips leading up to tax season, or advice on year-end financial planning. Timely content shows that you are on top of industry trends and are a reliable source of up-to-date information.

Creating value-driven content requires a deep understanding of your audience's needs and a commitment to providing useful, actionable information. By focusing on what your audience values, you can build a content strategy that not only attracts readers but also converts them into loyal clients.
  Leveraging Case Studies and Testimonials

Case studies and testimonials are powerful tools in your content strategy that can help build trust and credibility with your audience. They provide real-world examples of how your services have helped clients achieve their goals, solve problems, or overcome challenges. For accountants, leveraging these forms of content can be particularly effective in demonstrating your expertise and the tangible value you offer.

Leveraging Case Studies

Case studies are detailed accounts of how you have successfully helped a client with a specific issue or project. They allow potential clients to see your approach, the solutions you provided, and the results you achieved. Here's how to effectively use case studies in your content strategy:

1. Select the Right Clients: Choose clients whose stories will resonate with your target audience. For example, if your goal is to attract more small business owners, select case studies that highlight your work with small businesses rather than large corporations. Focus on cases that involve common challenges or concerns among your audience, such as tax issues, cash flow management, or navigating audits.

2. Outline the Problem and Solution Clearly: A good case study clearly outlines the client's problem, your approach to solving it, and the results achieved. Start by describing the client's situation and the challenges they were facing. Then, explain the specific steps you took to address these issues, and finally, highlight the positive outcomes. Use data and metrics to quantify the results whenever possible, such as "reduced tax liability by 25%" or "improved cash flow by $50,000."

3. Include Direct Quotes: Incorporate direct quotes from the client to add authenticity and a personal touch to your case study. These quotes can express the client's satisfaction with your services and highlight the impact you had on their business or financial situation. For example, a client might say, "Thanks to [Your Firm], we not only saved money on our taxes but also have a better understanding of our finances."

4. Use Visuals and Data: Enhance your case studies with visuals like charts, graphs, and before-and-after comparisons to make the results more tangible and engaging. Visual aids can help readers quickly grasp the significance of your work and the improvements achieved.

5. Make Them Accessible: Publish case studies on your website, ideally on a dedicated "Success Stories" or "Client Case Studies" page. You can also include them in proposals, presentations, or marketing materials. Ensure

they are easy to read and structured with headings, bullet points, and concise paragraphs to make the information digestible.

6. Promote Case Studies Across Channels: Share your case studies on social media, in your email newsletters, and on relevant pages of your website. They can also be used in webinars or speaking engagements as evidence of your expertise. The more visibility your case studies have, the more they can influence potential clients.

Leveraging Testimonials

Testimonials are shorter, more personal endorsements from clients that speak to their positive experiences working with your firm. They serve as social proof, showing that others have trusted and benefited from your services. Here's how to make the most of testimonials in your content strategy:

1. Request Testimonials from Satisfied Clients: After successfully completing a project, don't hesitate to ask your clients for a testimonial. Most satisfied clients are happy to provide a few sentences about their positive experience. Make it easy for them by providing a simple form or guiding them on what to include, such as specific aspects they appreciated about your service.

2. Highlight Specific Results or Benefits: The most effective testimonials go beyond general praise and highlight specific results or benefits. Instead of a generic statement like "Great service!", aim for more detailed feedback such as, "The team at [Your Firm] helped us streamline our bookkeeping processes, saving us hours of work each week and allowing us to focus on growing our business."

3. Use Real Names and Details: Whenever possible, include the client's name, company, and role in the testimonial. This adds credibility and makes the testimonial feel more authentic. If privacy is a concern, ask clients if they're comfortable with using just their first name or a more general description of

their business.

4. Place Testimonials Strategically: Place testimonials on key pages of your website, such as your homepage, service pages, and contact page, where they can reinforce your value proposition. A dedicated "Testimonials" page can also serve as a central repository for all client feedback.

5. Use Different Formats: Testimonials don't have to be just text. Consider using video testimonials, which can be more engaging and personal. A short video of a client sharing their positive experience can be highly impactful. If video isn't an option, consider adding client logos or photos alongside their written testimonials to add a visual element.

6. Regularly Update Your Testimonials: Keep your testimonials fresh by regularly adding new ones. This not only shows that you are actively helping clients but also reflects the current state of your business. Outdated testimonials can give the impression that your services are no longer relevant or that you haven't been active in the market.

Combining Case Studies and Testimonials

Using both case studies and testimonials together provides a comprehensive view of your capabilities and the satisfaction of your clients. While case studies offer detailed insights into how you solve specific problems, testimonials provide quick, personal endorsements that highlight your overall impact.

1. Create a Client Success Section: Consider creating a dedicated section on your website that combines case studies and testimonials. This "Client Success" section can serve as a powerful testament to your expertise and the quality of your services, making it easy for potential clients to see the value you provide.

2. Use Them in Your Sales Process: Case studies and testimonials are not just

for your website—they can be powerful tools in your sales process. Include them in proposals, presentations, or during consultations to demonstrate your track record of success. When prospects see that others have benefited from your services, they are more likely to trust you with their own needs.

3. Promote Through Multiple Channels: Share snippets of testimonials on social media, include them in email marketing campaigns, or feature them in digital ads. The more you can showcase your successes across different platforms, the more potential clients you can reach.

4. Tailor Them to Different Audience Segments: If you serve a diverse range of clients, tailor your case studies and testimonials to different audience segments. For example, if you work with both individuals and businesses, create separate case studies that cater to each group. This ensures that all potential clients can see examples that are relevant to their own needs.

A robust content strategy is essential for accountants who want to build their online presence, attract and retain clients, and establish themselves as trusted experts in their field. By developing a detailed content plan, choosing the right content formats, focusing on value-driven material, and effectively leveraging case studies and testimonials, you can create a content strategy that not only engages your audience but also drives tangible results for your accounting practice.

Remember, the key to a successful content strategy is consistency, relevance, and a clear focus on your audience's needs. Regularly assess the performance of your content, be open to making adjustments, and continue to evolve your strategy as your business and audience grow. By putting in the effort to create high-quality, targeted content, you can set your accounting firm apart in a competitive market and achieve lasting success.

Local SEO for Accountants

In an increasingly digital world, it's crucial for accountants to optimize their online presence to attract local clients. Local SEO (Search Engine Optimization) focuses on improving your visibility in local search results, helping potential clients in your area find your accounting services when they need them most. This chapter will cover why local SEO matters, how to optimize your Google My Business profile, the importance of local citations and directory listings, and how to gain positive online reviews.

Why Local SEO Matters

Local SEO is critical for accountants because most of your clients are likely to be within your local area. When someone searches for an accountant, they typically include location-specific keywords like "accountants near me" or "tax services in [City]." Optimizing for local SEO ensures that your firm appears prominently in these localized search results, driving more foot traffic, phone calls, and inquiries to your business.

1. Targeted Visibility: Local SEO targets people who are specifically looking for accounting services in your area. Unlike broad SEO, which can attract visitors from anywhere, local SEO focuses on reaching those who are geographically close to your business and more likely to become clients.

2. Higher Conversion Rates: People searching for local services are often closer to making a purchasing decision. For example, if someone searches for

"tax accountant near me," they are likely looking to hire an accountant soon. By appearing in local search results, you increase your chances of converting these searches into actual clients.

3. Competitive Advantage: Many accounting firms, especially smaller ones, overlook the importance of local SEO. By optimizing your local SEO, you can outperform competitors who are not taking advantage of these strategies, capturing a larger share of the local market.

4. Mobile Searches: With the rise of mobile devices, local searches have become more common. Many people search for services while on the go, using location-based queries. Google's algorithms prioritize local results for mobile users, making local SEO even more critical for reaching potential clients.

5. Building Trust and Credibility: Appearing in local search results, especially in Google's Local Pack (the top three local business listings displayed in a box on Google's search results), enhances your credibility. Potential clients are more likely to trust and choose a business that is prominently featured in local search results.

Local SEO is not just about being found; it's about being found by the right people—those who are actively looking for your services in your area. By focusing on local SEO, you can connect with these potential clients at the exact moment they need your services.

Optimizing Your Google My Business Profile

Google My Business (GMB) is a free tool that allows you to manage your business's online presence across Google, including Search and Maps. Optimizing your GMB profile is one of the most important steps in local SEO, as it directly influences your visibility in local search results. Here's how to optimize your Google My Business profile effectively:

1. Claim and Verify Your Business: The first step is to claim your business listing on Google My Business and verify it. Verification typically involves receiving a postcard with a verification code that you enter into your GMB account. This process confirms that your business is legitimate and located where you say it is.

2. Complete Your Profile: A complete and accurate GMB profile is more likely to rank higher in local search results. Make sure to fill out all the relevant information, including:
   - Business Name: Use your official business name without adding keywords or location-specific terms unless they are part of your legal business name.
   - Address: Provide a physical address that matches your business location. If you offer services at clients' locations, you can hide your address and specify a service area instead.
   - Phone Number: Use a local phone number that matches your business location. Avoid using toll-free numbers, as local numbers are better for local SEO.
   - Business Hours: List your regular business hours, and keep them updated. If you have special hours for holidays or tax season, make sure to reflect those changes.
   - Website: Link to your website's homepage or a specific landing page that provides more information about your services.

3. Choose the Right Categories: Selecting the right categories for your business is crucial, as it helps Google understand what your business does. Choose primary and secondary categories that best describe your services, such as "Accountant," "Tax Consultant," or "Bookkeeping Service."

4. Write a Compelling Business Description: Your business description should clearly and concisely explain what your accounting firm offers and what sets you apart from competitors. Focus on your key services, expertise, and any specializations. For example, "We provide comprehensive tax planning and preparation services for small businesses in [City], with over 20

years of experience in the industry."

5. Add High-Quality Photos: Photos make your GMB profile more engaging and can help attract more clicks. Include professional photos of your office, team members, and any relevant branding materials. Update your photos regularly to keep your profile fresh.

6. Encourage Reviews: Positive reviews on your GMB profile can significantly impact your local SEO rankings. Encourage satisfied clients to leave reviews, and respond to reviews—both positive and negative—in a timely and professional manner. Engaging with reviews shows that you value customer feedback and are committed to providing excellent service.

7. Post Regular Updates: Google My Business allows you to post updates about your business, such as special offers, events, or new services. Regularly posting updates keeps your profile active and can improve your visibility in local searches.

8. Use the Messaging Feature: Google My Business offers a messaging feature that allows potential clients to contact you directly through your GMB profile. Enable this feature and ensure that you or your team respond to inquiries promptly.

By optimizing your Google My Business profile, you can increase your visibility in local searches, attract more clients, and build trust with your audience.

Local Citations and Directory Listings

Local citations and directory listings refer to mentions of your business's name, address, and phone number (NAP) on other websites, typically in local directories or business listings. These citations help establish your business's credibility and improve your local SEO rankings. Here's how to manage and optimize local citations effectively:

1. Consistency is Key: Ensure that your NAP information is consistent across all citations and directory listings. Inconsistencies, such as different addresses or phone numbers, can confuse search engines and reduce your local SEO effectiveness. Double-check that your business name, address, and phone number are identical on every platform.

2. Submit to Reputable Directories: Focus on submitting your business to reputable and relevant local directories. Start with major platforms like Yelp, Yellow Pages, and Bing Places, and then expand to industry-specific directories, such as accounting association directories. Local chambers of commerce or business associations also often have directories where you can list your business.

3. Claim and Manage Listings: Claim your business listings on major directory sites to ensure you have control over the information presented. Once claimed, you can update your business information, add photos, respond to reviews, and make other improvements that enhance your online presence.

4. Build Citations on High-Authority Sites: Not all citations are created equal. Citations on high-authority sites, such as Google My Business, Yelp, and industry-specific directories, carry more weight and can have a more significant impact on your local SEO. Focus on building citations on these platforms to boost your rankings.

5. Monitor and Clean Up Inaccurate Citations: Over time, your business may accumulate inaccurate or outdated citations. Use tools like Moz Local, Bright Local, or Yext to audit your citations and identify any that are incorrect or duplicated. Work to clean up these citations to ensure they are accurate and consistent.

6. Encourage Mentions from Local Media: Local media outlets, such as newspapers, magazines, and online news sites, often feature businesses in their coverage. Getting mentioned in local media can act as a powerful citation, boosting your local SEO and credibility. Build relationships with local journalists and pitch stories that highlight your expertise or community involvement.

7. Leverage Social Media Profiles: Social media profiles on platforms like Facebook, LinkedIn, and Twitter also count as citations. Ensure that your NAP information is accurate and consistent on all social media profiles. Regularly update your social media pages with relevant content to keep them active and engaging.

Local citations and directory listings are essential for improving your local search rankings and establishing your business's online presence. By managing these citations carefully, you can enhance your visibility in local searches and attract more clients in your area.

Gaining Positive Online Reviews

Online reviews play a significant role in local SEO and can influence potential clients' decisions to use your services. Positive reviews not only boost your credibility but also improve your rankings in local search results. Here's how to encourage and manage positive online reviews for your accounting firm:

1. Provide Exceptional Service: The foundation of positive reviews is exceptional service. When clients have a great experience with your firm, they are more likely to leave positive feedback. Focus on providing high-quality services, being responsive to client needs, and maintaining clear communication.

2. Ask for Reviews: Don't be afraid to ask satisfied clients to leave reviews. Timing is important—ask for a review shortly after a successful project or

positive interaction when the client is most likely to be pleased with your services. You can ask in person, via email, or through follow-up surveys.

3. Make It Easy: Simplify the process of leaving a review by providing direct links to your review profiles on Google, Yelp, or other relevant platforms. Include these links in your email signatures, on your website, and in follow-up communications. The easier it is for clients to leave a review, the more likely they are to do so.

4. Respond to Reviews: Engage with your reviews by responding to them promptly and professionally. For positive reviews, thank the reviewer for their feedback and express appreciation for their business. For negative reviews, respond calmly and professionally, offering to resolve the issue offline if possible. Demonstrating that you care about client feedback can help build trust and show potential clients that you are committed to providing excellent service.

5. Highlight Positive Reviews: Showcase positive reviews on your website, in marketing materials, and on your social media profiles. This not only builds credibility but also encourages other clients to leave their own feedback. A dedicated testimonials or reviews page on your website can serve as a powerful tool for building trust with potential clients.

6. Monitor Your Online Reputation: Regularly monitor your online reviews across various platforms to stay on top of what clients are saying about your business. Use tools like Google Alerts, Review Trackers, or other reputation management tools to receive notifications of new reviews and respond accordingly.

7. Avoid Fake Reviews: Resist the temptation to use fake reviews or pay for reviews, as this can backfire and damage your reputation. Most review platforms have strict policies against fake reviews, and violations can lead to penalties, including removal of reviews or even suspension of your business

listing. Focus on building genuine reviews from real clients who have had positive experiences with your firm.

8. Encourage Reviews on Multiple Platforms: While Google reviews are critical for local SEO, it's also beneficial to gather reviews on other platforms like Yelp, Facebook, and industry-specific sites. A diverse range of reviews across multiple platforms strengthens your online presence and increases your visibility in local searches.

Positive online reviews are a powerful component of local SEO, helping to build trust with potential clients and improve your rankings in local search results. By encouraging reviews, responding to feedback, and highlighting positive experiences, you can leverage reviews to enhance your online reputation and attract more local clients.

Link Building Strategies

Link building is a fundamental aspect of SEO that involves acquiring hyperlinks from other websites to your own. These back links are seen as votes of confidence by search engines, indicating that your content is valuable and authoritative. For accountants, building high-quality links can significantly improve your search engine rankings, increase traffic, and enhance your online credibility. In this chapter, we'll explore the importance of back links, how to get high-quality links, avoiding black hat SEO practices, and networking and outreach strategies for link building.

The Importance of Back links

Back links are crucial for SEO because they serve as endorsements from other websites, signaling to search engines that your content is trustworthy and relevant. High-quality back links can boost your site's authority and improve your rankings in search results. Here's why back links are essential for accountants:

1. Improves Search Engine Rankings: Back links are one of the top-ranking factors for search engines like Google. The more high-quality back links you have pointing to your site, the more likely it is that search engines will rank your pages higher in search results.

2. Drives Referral Traffic: Back links not only help with SEO but also drive referral traffic from other websites. When a reputable site links to your

content, their audience can click through to your site, potentially converting into clients.

3. Builds Authority and Trust: High-quality back links from authoritative websites help establish your site's credibility and authority in your field. For accountants, links from reputable sources like financial blogs, business directories, and industry publications can enhance your professional image.

4. Increases Indexing Rates: Back links help search engine crawlers find your site more easily. When a search engine bot crawls a site that links to yours, it follows the link and discovers your pages, leading to faster indexing and improved visibility in search results.

5. Enhances Brand Visibility: Back links from popular sites increase your brand's exposure to a broader audience. This increased visibility can lead to more recognition and awareness of your accounting firm, further establishing you as an industry leader.

How to Get High-Quality Links

Getting high-quality back links involves earning links naturally through valuable content, building relationships, and engaging in strategic outreach. Here are some effective strategies for acquiring high-quality back links for your accounting website:

1. Create Link-Worthy Content: The foundation of any successful link-building strategy is creating high-quality, valuable content that others want to link to. This can include in-depth guides, informative blog posts, industry reports, info graphics, and case studies. Focus on creating content that addresses common pain points, provides unique insights, or offers actionable advice for your target audience.

2. Guest Blogging: Guest blogging involves writing articles for other websites

in your industry. By contributing valuable content to reputable sites, you can earn back links in return. Look for opportunities to guest blog on financial websites, business blogs, or industry publications that cater to your target audience. Ensure that your guest posts are relevant, informative, and provide value to the host site's readers.

3. Leverage Local Partnerships: Form partnerships with local businesses, associations, or community organizations that are willing to link to your site. For example, you could sponsor a local event, collaborate on a community project, or provide expert advice to a local business group, all of which can result in back links.

4. Use Broken Link Building: Broken link building involves finding broken links on other websites and suggesting your content as a replacement. Use tools like Ahrefs or Check My Links to identify broken links on relevant websites. Reach out to the site owners, inform them of the broken link, and offer your content as a suitable replacement. This strategy not only helps you earn a back link but also provides value to the website owner by helping them fix a broken link.

5. Participate in Industry Forums and Q&A Sites: Engage in industry forums, Q&A sites like Quora, or community platforms where you can provide expert answers and advice. Include links to relevant content on your website when it's appropriate and helpful to the discussion. Be mindful not to spam; your primary goal should be to add value to the conversation.

6. Create and Promote Info graphics: Info graphics are highly shareable and can attract back links from websites looking to include visual content. Create info graphics that simplify complex accounting topics or present interesting data related to your industry. Promote your info graphics on social media, relevant blogs, and info graphic directories to increase visibility and earn back links.

7. Reach Out to Influences and Bloggers: Identify influences, bloggers, or industry experts who write about topics related to accounting. Build relationships with them through social media engagement, commenting on their posts, and sharing their content. Once you've established a connection, you can reach out and suggest content on your site that might be of interest to their audience.

8. List Your Business in Relevant Directories: In addition to local citations, listing your business in reputable online directories can also earn back links. Look for industry-specific directories, such as those for accounting professionals or financial services, and ensure that your business information is accurate and up-to-date.

Avoiding Black Hat SEO Practices

While building back links is crucial for SEO, it's important to avoid black hat SEO practices that can lead to penalties from search engines. Black hat SEO refers to unethical techniques that attempt to manipulate search engine rankings, often resulting in short-term gains but long-term damage. Here's what to avoid:

1. Buying Links: Purchasing back links from link farms or low-quality sites is against Google's guidelines and can result in severe penalties. Instead of buying links, focus on earning them through legitimate strategies like content creation and outreach.

2. Using Private Blog Networks (PBNs): PBNs are groups of websites created solely for the purpose of linking to each other and manipulating search rankings. Search engines can detect PBNs, and using them can lead to penalties or even removal from search results.

3. Spamming Comments and Forums: Avoid leaving spammy links in comments or forums that have no relevance to the discussion. Not only

is this ineffective, but it also damages your reputation and can result in your links being flagged as spam.

4. Excessive Reciprocal Linking: Reciprocal linking, or exchanging links with other websites, is fine in moderation but can be problematic if overused. Excessive reciprocal linking appears unnatural and can be flagged by search engines. Focus on earning links organically rather than through link exchanges.

5. Cloaking and Link Schemes: Cloaking involves presenting different content to search engines and users, while link schemes involve manipulative practices like hiding links or using unrelated anchor text. Both are considered black hat tactics and can lead to penalties.

By avoiding these black hat SEO practices and focusing on ethical, white hat link-building strategies, you can build a strong, sustainable back link profile that supports your long-term SEO goals.

Networking and Outreach for Link Building

Building relationships and conducting outreach are key components of successful link-building strategies. Networking with other professionals, bloggers, and industry leaders can open doors to new link-building opportunities. Here's how to effectively network and conduct outreach for link building:

1. Build Relationships in Your Industry: Attend industry events, webinars, and networking groups to connect with other professionals in your field. Building relationships with other accountants, financial advisors, and business owners can lead to natural link-building opportunities, such as guest blogging or collaborative content.

2. Personalize Your Outreach: When reaching out to websites for link-

building opportunities, personalize your messages. Show that you've done your research, understand their audience, and have a genuine interest in contributing value. Personalized outreach is more likely to receive positive responses than generic, templated emails.

3. Offer Value First: When networking and conducting outreach, focus on offering value rather than just asking for a link. Provide useful insights, share resources, or offer to collaborate on a project. By building a reputation as a valuable contributor, you increase the likelihood of earning back links in return.

4. Leverage Social Media and Professional Networks: Use social media platforms like LinkedIn, Twitter, and Facebook to connect with influences, bloggers, and potential link partners. Share your content, engage in discussions, and showcase your expertise. By being active on social media, you can expand your network and increase your visibility, making it easier for others to discover and link to your content.

5. Follow Up Politely: If you don't receive a response to your initial outreach, it's okay to follow up after a week or two. Keep your follow-up messages polite and brief, and reiterate the value of your content or the collaboration you're proposing. Persistence can pay off, but it's important not to be pushy or overly aggressive.

6. Create Collaborative Content: Partner with other professionals or businesses in your industry to create collaborative content, such as co-authored articles, joint webinars, or round-up posts featuring expert opinions. Collaborative content is more likely to be shared and linked to by multiple parties, amplifying your reach and link-building potential.

7. Utilize Press Releases: Press releases can be an effective way to announce major news, such as a new service offering, a partnership, or a significant milestone for your accounting firm. Distributing press releases through

reputable channels can attract the attention of journalists and bloggers, leading to media coverage and back links.

8. Offer to Be a Source: Platforms like Help a Reporter Out (HARO) connect journalists with experts who can provide insights or quotes for their articles. By offering your expertise as an accountant, you can earn mentions and back links from high-authority media outlets. This not only builds your back link profile but also enhances your reputation as an industry expert.

9. Monitor and Capitalize on Brand Mentions: Use tools like Google Alerts or Mention to monitor when your brand or content is mentioned online. If you come across unlinked mentions of your business, reach out to the site owner and request a link back to your website. Since they've already mentioned your brand, they may be more receptive to adding a link.

10. Create Shareable Content: Content that is highly shareable, such as info graphics, tools, templates, or interactive calculators, can naturally attract back links. For accountants, creating tools like tax calculators, budget planners, or downloadable templates for financial statements can be particularly useful. Shareable content provides immediate value and is more likely to be referenced by other websites.

11. Participate in Podcasts and Webinars: Being a guest on podcasts or participating in webinars is a great way to share your expertise and reach a wider audience. These platforms often include back links to your website in the show notes or webinar resources, providing both exposure and valuable links.

12. Maintain Long-Term Relationships: Successful link building is not just about one-time transactions; it's about building long-term relationships with others in your industry. Stay in touch with your link partners, continue to offer value, and be open to future collaborations. Building a network of supportive peers can lead to ongoing link-building opportunities that benefit

both parties.

Link building is a critical component of any effective SEO strategy, especially for accountants who want to enhance their online presence, improve search engine rankings, and attract more clients. By focusing on ethical, white hat link-building strategies, such as creating valuable content, engaging in guest blogging, leveraging local partnerships, and conducting targeted outreach, you can build a strong and sustainable back link profile.

Avoiding black hat SEO practices and instead prioritizing quality over quantity will ensure that your link-building efforts contribute positively to your long-term success. Networking, outreach, and relationship-building are the keys to earning high-quality back links that not only boost your SEO but also enhance your reputation and authority in the accounting industry.

By integrating these link-building strategies into your overall SEO plan, you can achieve greater visibility, drive more traffic, and ultimately grow your accounting firm in a competitive digital landscape. Remember, link building is an ongoing process that requires persistence, creativity, and a commitment to providing value to your audience and peers. With the right approach, link building can be a powerful tool in your SEO arsenal, helping you reach new heights in your business.

SEO Tools and Resources

SEO (Search Engine Optimization) is essential for improving your website's visibility on search engines like Google. To make the most of your SEO efforts, it's important to use the right tools and resources. This chapter will provide an overview of essential SEO tools, explain how to use Google Analytics for SEO, compare free and paid SEO tools, and offer tips on staying updated with the latest SEO trends. By the end, you'll have a clear understanding of how to leverage these tools to enhance your website's performance and drive more traffic to your business.

Overview of Essential SEO Tools

There are countless SEO tools available that can help you improve your website's search engine ranking. These tools can assist you in various aspects of SEO, such as keyword research, on-page optimization, back link analysis, and performance tracking. Below are some of the most essential SEO tools that every business should consider using:

1. Google Analytics: Google Analytics is a free tool that tracks and reports website traffic. It provides insights into how visitors find and interact with your site, which pages they visit, how long they stay, and what actions they take. This data is crucial for understanding your audience and optimizing your site's performance.

2. Google Search Console: This is another free tool from Google that helps

you monitor and maintain your site's presence in Google search results. It provides information about your site's indexing status, search queries that bring traffic, crawl errors, and back links. It's essential for identifying and fixing issues that could impact your SEO.

3. Ahrefs: Ahrefs is a powerful paid tool known for its back link analysis and keyword research capabilities. It provides detailed insights into your competitors' SEO strategies, helping you find opportunities to improve your own rankings. Ahrefs also offers tools for site audits, rank tracking, and content analysis.

4. SEMrush: SEMrush is a comprehensive SEO tool that offers features like keyword research, competitor analysis, rank tracking, and site auditing. It's popular for its user-friendly interface and in-depth data, making it a great choice for businesses looking to optimize their digital marketing strategies.

5. Moz Pro: Moz Pro is another well-known SEO tool that provides keyword research, link building, and site auditing features. It's particularly useful for its domain authority metrics, which help you understand how your site's authority compares to your competitors.

6. Yoast SEO: If you use WordPress, Yoast SEO is a must-have plugin that helps you optimize your content for search engines. It provides real-time feedback on your content's readability, keyword usage, and technical SEO elements like meta tags and sitemaps.

7. Screaming Frog SEO Spider: Screaming Frog is a desktop application that crawls your website, identifying issues like broken links, duplicate content, and missing meta tags. It's an excellent tool for conducting detailed site audits and identifying technical SEO problems that need fixing.

8. Ubersuggest: Developed by Neil Patel, Ubersuggest is a free and easy-to-use tool for keyword research, site audits, and back link analysis. It's great for

beginners who need basic SEO insights without the cost of more advanced tools.

9. Google Page Speed Insights: This tool analyzes your website's speed and provides suggestions for improving load times. Site speed is a critical factor for SEO, as faster websites provide a better user experience and rank higher in search results.

10. AnswerThePublic: This tool helps you understand what questions people are asking online about specific topics. It's useful for generating content ideas and targeting keywords that match user intent.

Each of these tools serves a specific purpose within the broader scope of SEO. By using them together you can gain a comprehensive understanding of your site's performance, identify areas for improvement, and implement effective SEO strategies.

How to Use Google Analytics for SEO

Google Analytics is a powerful tool that provides valuable insights into your website's performance. Understanding how to use Google Analytics effectively can significantly enhance your SEO efforts. Here's a simple guide on how to leverage Google Analytics for SEO:

1. Setting Up Google Analytics: To get started, you need to create a Google Analytics account and add your website as a property. You'll receive a tracking code that needs to be added to your website's header. Once set up, Google Analytics will begin collecting data about your site's visitors and their behavior.

2. Tracking Traffic Sources: In Google Analytics, navigate to "Acquisition" > "All Traffic" > "Channels." Here, you can see where your traffic is coming from, including organic search, direct traffic, social media, and referrals. This

information helps you understand how well your SEO efforts are driving traffic compared to other channels.

3. Monitoring Keyword Performance: Under "Acquisition" > "Search Console" > "Queries," you can view the search terms that are bringing visitors to your site. This data helps you identify which keywords are performing well and which ones may need more optimization.

4. Analyzing User Behavior: The "Behavior" section in Google Analytics provides insights into how visitors interact with your site. You can see which pages are most popular, how long visitors stay on your site, and what actions they take. This information is useful for identifying content that resonates with your audience and pages that may need improvement.

5. Tracking Bounce Rate: Bounce rate refers to the percentage of visitors who leave your site after viewing only one page. A high bounce rate can indicate that your content isn't meeting user expectations or that there are technical issues like slow load times. Use Google Analytics to monitor bounce rates and identify pages that need optimization.

6. Setting Up Goals: Goals in Google Analytics allow you to track specific actions that you want visitors to take, such as filling out a contact form or signing up for a newsletter. Setting up goals helps you measure the effectiveness of your SEO efforts in driving conversions.

7. Using the Site Speed Report: Site speed is a crucial factor for both user experience and SEO. Google Analytics provides a "Site Speed" report under the "Behavior" section, which shows how quickly your pages are loading. If you notice slow load times, take steps to optimize images, enable browser caching, or improve server response times.

8. Analyzing Mobile Traffic: With mobile searches on the rise, it's important to ensure your site performs well on mobile devices. The "Audience" >

"Mobile" > "Overview" report shows how much of your traffic comes from mobile devices and how those users behave on your site. Use this data to optimize your site for mobile, ensuring a seamless experience across all devices.

By using Google Analytics effectively, you can gain a deeper understanding of your website's performance and make data-driven decisions to improve your SEO efforts.

Free vs. Paid SEO Tools: What You Need

There are both free and paid SEO tools available, each with its own set of features and benefits. Choosing the right tools depends on your budget, the complexity of your SEO needs, and your level of expertise. Here's a comparison of free vs. paid SEO tools to help you decide what you need:

1. Free SEO Tools:
   - Pros: Free tools like Google Analytics, Google Search Console, Ubersuggest, and Moz's free features provide basic SEO insights without any cost. They are great for small businesses, beginners, or those on a tight budget. These tools offer essential features like keyword research, site audits, and traffic analysis.
   - Cons: Free tools often have limitations in terms of data depth, accuracy, and the number of queries you can run. They may not provide the advanced features needed for comprehensive SEO strategies, such as detailed competitor analysis, extensive back link tracking, or sophisticated reporting.

2. Paid SEO Tools:
   - Pros: Paid tools like Ahrefs, SEMrush, and Moz Pro offer advanced features that go beyond what free tools provide. These tools include in-depth keyword research, competitive analysis, rank tracking, back link monitoring, and comprehensive site audits. They also offer more robust data, better accuracy, and a wider range of metrics.

- Cons: The main drawback of paid tools is the cost, which can range from $50 to several hundred dollars per month. For small businesses or those just starting with SEO, this can be a significant investment. It's important to evaluate whether the advanced features are necessary for your specific needs.

3. Which Should You Choose?:
   - If you're new to SEO or running a small business, start with free tools to get a basic understanding of your site's performance. As your SEO efforts grow and you need more advanced insights, consider investing in a paid tool that aligns with your goals.

- Evaluate your needs: If your primary focus is on keyword research, a tool like Ubersuggest or Google Keyword Planner might suffice. However, if you need a full suite of SEO capabilities, a paid tool like Ahrefs or SEMrush would be more suitable.

Both free and paid tools have their place in a successful SEO strategy. By starting with free options and gradually incorporating paid tools as your needs evolve, you can build an effective SEO toolkit that supports your business goals.

Staying Updated with SEO Trends

SEO is constantly evolving, with search engine algorithms frequently changing and new techniques emerging. Staying updated with the latest SEO trends is crucial for maintaining your site's performance and staying ahead of the competition. Here are some tips on how to keep up with SEO trends:

1. Follow Industry Blogs and News Sites: Websites like Moz, Search Engine Journal, and Search Engine Land regularly publish articles on the latest SEO trends, updates, and best practices. Subscribing to their newsletters or following them on social media can keep you informed about the newest

developments in SEO.

2. Join SEO Communities and Forums: Online communities like Reddit's r/SEO, SEO-focused Facebook groups, and industry forums provide valuable insights and discussions on current SEO trends and challenges. Engaging in these communities allows you to learn from other professionals, ask questions, and share your experiences.

3. Attend Webinars and Conferences: SEO webinars and conferences are excellent ways to learn from experts and gain in-depth knowledge about the latest SEO strategies. Events like MozCon, SMX (Search Marketing Expo), and Brighton bring together industry leaders who share their insights on what's working in SEO today.

4. Follow SEO Experts on Social Media: Many SEO experts regularly share updates, tips, and industry news on platforms like Twitter and LinkedIn. Following influences such as Rand Fishkin, Neil Patel, and Barry Schwartz can provide you with real-time updates and expert perspectives on SEO trends.

5. Subscribe to SEO Newsletters: Newsletters from SEO tools like Ahrefs, SEMrush, and Moz often include curated content about the latest SEO changes, case studies, and new strategies. Subscribing to these newsletters can help you stay informed without having to constantly search for information.

6. Experiment and Test: SEO is not one-size-fits-all, and what works for one site may not work for another. Regularly experiment with different strategies and test their impact on your site's performance. Use A/B testing for changes in content, meta tags, or layout to see what yields the best results for your audience.

7. Keep Up with Google's Algorithm Updates: Google frequently updates its search algorithms, which can significantly impact SEO strategies. Major

updates are often announced on Google's official blogs or Twitter accounts. Understanding these updates helps you adjust your tactics to align with the latest ranking factors.

8. Use SEO Tools for Insights: Many SEO tools, such as Ahrefs and SEMrush, have built-in features that provide alerts on new trends and algorithm changes. Utilize these alerts to stay on top of any developments that may affect your SEO efforts.

9. Participate in Online Courses and Certifications: Many platforms offer SEO courses that cover both basic and advanced topics. Websites like Coursera, Hub Spot Academy, and Google's Digital Garage provide courses that can help you enhance your SEO skills and stay updated with the latest best practices.

10. Set Up Google Alerts: Google Alerts is a simple tool that can notify you of new content related to specific keywords. Set up alerts for terms like "SEO trends" or "Google algorithm update" to receive notifications about the latest developments in your inbox.

Conclusion

Using the right SEO tools and resources is essential for improving your website's search engine performance and driving more traffic to your business. By leveraging essential tools like Google Analytics and Google Search Console, you can gain valuable insights into your site's performance and make data-driven decisions to enhance your SEO efforts. Understanding the difference between free and paid tools allows you to choose the ones that best fit your needs and budget.

Staying updated with SEO trends is also crucial, as the SEO landscape is constantly evolving. By following industry experts, participating in online communities, attending webinars, and regularly testing new strategies, you can keep your SEO approach current and effective.

SEO is an ongoing process that requires consistent effort and adaptation. By equipping yourself with the right tools, staying informed about the latest trends, and continuously refining your strategies, you can achieve long-term success in your SEO efforts and grow your accounting business in the digital marketplace.

Tracking Your SEO Performance*

Tracking your SEO performance is essential for understanding how well your efforts are paying off and where you need to make adjustments. By monitoring key metrics, setting up regular SEO reports, analyzing traffic and conversions, and making data-driven adjustments, you can continuously improve your website's visibility and effectiveness. This chapter will guide you through the process of tracking your SEO performance, from understanding which metrics matter most to using data to refine your strategy.

Key SEO Metrics to Monitor

To effectively track your SEO performance, you need to focus on specific metrics that give you a clear picture of how your website is doing. Here are the key SEO metrics you should monitor regularly:

1. Organic Traffic: Organic traffic refers to visitors who find your website through search engines like Google without clicking on paid ads. This metric shows how well your SEO efforts are working to attract visitors. You can track organic traffic using Google Analytics by looking at the "Acquisition" > "All Traffic" > "Channels" report and focusing on the "Organic Search" section.

2. Keyword Rankings: Monitoring where your website ranks for important keywords helps you understand your visibility in search engine results. Use tools like Google Search Console, Ahrefs, or SEMrush to track the positions

of your target keywords over time. Improving your rankings for relevant keywords can lead to more traffic and potential clients.

3. Click-Through Rate (CTR): CTR measures the percentage of users who click on your link when it appears in search results. A higher CTR indicates that your meta titles and descriptions are effective at capturing interest. You can find CTR data in Google Search Console under the "Performance" report. Improving your CTR can lead to increased traffic without necessarily changing your rankings.

4. Bounce Rate: Bounce rate is the percentage of visitors who leave your website after viewing only one page. A high bounce rate may indicate that users are not finding what they are looking for or that your site has usability issues. You can track bounce rates in Google Analytics under the "Audience" > "Overview" section. Reducing bounce rates can help improve user engagement and conversions.

5. Pages Per Session: This metric shows how many pages, on average, a visitor views during a single session on your site. A higher number suggests that users are exploring your content and finding it valuable. You can find this data in Google Analytics under "Behavior" > "Overview." Encouraging users to visit more pages can improve their experience and increase the likelihood of conversions.

6. Average Session Duration: Average session duration measures how long visitors stay on your site during a visit. Longer sessions usually indicate that your content is engaging and valuable. This metric is available in Google Analytics under "Audience" > "Overview." Increasing session duration can help improve your site's overall performance and user satisfaction.

7. Conversion Rate: Conversion rate measures the percentage of visitors who complete a desired action, such as filling out a contact form, signing up for a newsletter, or making a purchase. Tracking conversions is critical for

understanding the effectiveness of your SEO in driving business results. Set up goals in Google Analytics to track specific conversions relevant to your business.

8. Back links: Back links are links from other websites that point to your site. They are a key factor in search engine rankings and help build your site's authority. Tools like Ahrefs, Moz, and SEMrush can help you monitor your back link profile, showing how many back links you have, their quality, and where they come from.

9. Page Load Time: Page load time is the time it takes for your web pages to fully load. Faster load times contribute to a better user experience and can positively impact your SEO rankings. Use Google Page Speed Insights or the "Site Speed" report in Google Analytics to monitor and optimize your page load times.

10. Indexed Pages: The number of pages indexed by search engines indicates how much of your site is visible to search engine users. You can check indexed pages in Google Search Console under the "Coverage" report. Regularly monitoring indexed pages helps you ensure that important content is being found by search engines.

By consistently monitoring these key SEO metrics, you can gain valuable insights into your website's performance and identify areas for improvement.

Setting Up SEO Reports

SEO reports are essential for tracking your progress, communicating results to stakeholders, and making data-driven decisions. Setting up regular SEO reports allows you to keep an eye on the most important metrics and adjust your strategy as needed. Here's how to set up effective SEO reports:

1. Define Your Objectives: Before creating an SEO report, it's important

TRACKING YOUR SEO PERFORMANCE*

to define what you want to achieve with your SEO efforts. Are you focusing on increasing organic traffic, improving keyword rankings, boosting conversions, or all of the above? Clearly defining your objectives will help you determine which metrics to include in your report.

2. Choose the Right Tools: Several tools can help you create SEO reports, including Google Analytics, Google Search Console, Ahrefs, SEMrush, and Moz. These tools provide customizable reporting features that allow you to track key metrics and generate detailed reports. Google Data Studio is also a great option for creating visually appealing reports that integrate data from multiple sources.

3. Set a Reporting Schedule: Consistency is key when it comes to SEO reporting. Decide how often you will generate reports—whether it's weekly, monthly, or quarterly—based on your needs and objectives. Regular reporting helps you track progress over time and identify trends or issues early on.

4. Include Key Metrics: Your SEO report should include the key metrics that align with your goals. For example, if your goal is to increase organic traffic, include metrics like organic traffic growth, keyword rankings, and CTR. If conversions are your focus, include metrics like conversion rate, goal completions, and OI.

5. Visualize Your Data: Use charts, graphs, and tables to present your data in a clear and easy-to-understand format. Visual representations make it easier to identify trends, compare performance over time, and communicate results to stakeholders. Google Data Studio, Excel, and Google Sheets offer various visualization options for your reports.

6. Provide Insights and Recommendations: Don't just present data—interpret it. Highlight key insights, such as significant changes in traffic or rankings, and provide actionable recommendations for improvement. For example, if you notice a drop in traffic from a specific keyword, suggest ways to optimize

content or adjust your keyword strategy.

7. Keep It Simple: Avoid overwhelming your audience with too much information. Focus on the most important metrics and insights that align with your goals. A concise, well-structured report is more effective than a lengthy one filled with unnecessary data.

8. Track Progress Over Time: Include comparisons to previous periods (e.g., month-over-month or year-over-year) to show progress and trends. Tracking performance over time helps you see the impact of your SEO efforts and identify any seasonal patterns or anomalies.

Setting up regular SEO reports allows you to track your performance, measure success, and make informed decisions that drive your SEO strategy forward.

Analyzing Traffic, Conversions, and ROI

Analyzing your traffic, conversions, and return on investment (ROI) is critical for understanding the effectiveness of your SEO efforts and determining whether they are delivering the desired results. Here's how to analyze these key aspects of your SEO performance:

1. Analyzing Traffic:
   - Organic vs. Other Traffic Sources: In Google Analytics, go to "Acquisition" > "All Traffic" > "Channels" to compare organic traffic to other sources like direct, referral, and social traffic. This analysis helps you understand how much of your traffic is driven by SEO compared to other marketing efforts.
   - Top Landing Pages: Identify which pages are attracting the most organic traffic by navigating to "Behavior" > "Site Content" > "Landing Pages." Analyzing top landing pages shows you which content is resonating with your audience and where you may need to focus optimization efforts.
   - Traffic Trends Over Time: Use the "Date Range" feature in Google

TRACKING YOUR SEO PERFORMANCE*

Analytics to compare traffic trends over different time periods. Look for patterns, spikes, or drops in traffic and investigate potential causes, such as algorithm updates, seasonal changes, or changes in your SEO strategy.

2. Analyzing Conversions:

   - Setting Up Goals: Set up goals in Google Analytics to track key actions that indicate a successful conversion, such as contact form submissions, newsletter sign-ups, or purchases. Go to "Admin" > "Goals" > "New Goal" to create specific goals based on your business objectives.

   - Conversion Rate Analyze your conversion rate to see what percentage of visitors are taking the desired action. A low conversion rate may indicate that your landing pages need optimization or that your content isn't aligning with user intent. Find this data in Google Analytics under "Conversions" > "Goals" > "Overview."

   - Conversion by Channel: To see how different channels contribute to conversions, go to "Conversions" > "Multi-Channel Funnels" > "Assisted Conversions." This report shows how different marketing channels, including organic search, play a role in driving conversions.

3. Calculating ROI:

   - Define Your Investment: Calculate the total investment in your SEO efforts, including costs for tools, content creation, and any outsourced services. This gives you a clear picture of how much you're spending on SEO.

   - Measure Revenue from SEO: Determine how much revenue can be attributed to SEO-driven conversions. For example, if your SEO efforts lead to a new client who generates $5,000 in revenue, you can attribute that amount to your SEO ROI.

   - Calculate ROI: Use the formula:

   ROI = (Revenue from SEO - Cost of SEO) / Cost of SEO x 100

   A positive ROI indicates that your SEO efforts are paying off, while a negative ROI suggests that you may need to reevaluate your strategy. Understanding your ROI helps you make informed decisions about where to allocate resources and whether to scale up or adjust your SEO investments.

4. Attribution Models: Use attribution models in Google Analytics to understand how different touch points contribute to conversions. The default model, "Last Interaction," attributes 100% of the conversion value to the last channel the user interacted with before converting. However, other models like "First Interaction" or "Linear" spread the value across multiple touch points, giving you a fuller picture of how SEO plays a role in the conversion journey.

By thoroughly analyzing traffic, conversions, and ROI, you can gain a clear understanding of how your SEO efforts impact your overall business performance. This data-driven approach allows you to make smarter decisions that align with your business goals.

Adjusting Your Strategy Based on Data

Tracking and analyzing your SEO performance is only the beginning. The real value comes from using this data to adjust your strategy and continuously improve your results. Here's how to adjust your SEO strategy based on the insights you gather:

1. Identify Areas for Improvement: Use your SEO reports and analysis to pinpoint areas that need attention. For example, if you notice that a particular keyword's ranking has dropped, investigate the cause and make necessary changes, such as updating content, adding new back links, or improving on-page optimization.

2. Test and Experiment: SEO is not an exact science, and what works for one site may not work for another. Continuously test different approaches, such as changing your meta descriptions to improve CTR, experimenting with different types of content, or adjusting your internal linking structure. Use A/B testing tools to compare changes and measure their impact on

performance.

3. Focus on High-Performing Content: Identify which content pieces are driving the most traffic, engagement, and conversions. Consider expanding on these topics, creating related content, or updating existing posts to keep them relevant. Leveraging high-performing content can help you capitalize on what's already working well.

4. Address Technical SEO Issues: Regularly review your site's technical health using tools like Google Search Console and Screaming Frog. Fix any identified issues, such as broken links, slow page load times, or mobile usability problems. Addressing technical issues ensures that your site remains accessible and optimized for both users and search engines.

5. Refine Your Keyword Strategy: Analyze keyword performance data to refine your strategy. If certain keywords are not performing as expected, consider targeting different keywords with less competition or better alignment with user intent. Use tools like Ahrefs or SEMrush to find new keyword opportunities based on your data analysis.

6. Monitor Competitors: Keep an eye on your competitors' SEO performance to identify new strategies or tactics you can adopt. Tools like Ahrefs and SEMrush allow you to track competitors' rankings, back link profiles, and content strategies. Understanding what your competitors are doing well can inspire new ideas and adjustments to your own strategy.

7. Adjust Based on Algorithm Changes: Search engine algorithms are constantly evolving, and changes can impact your rankings. Stay informed about major updates by following industry news and monitoring your site's performance during and after updates. If you notice a drop in rankings, review the latest algorithm changes and adjust your strategy accordingly.

8. Set New Goals and Benchmarks: As you achieve your SEO goals, set

new ones to continue driving growth. For example, if you've successfully increased organic traffic, your next goal might be to improve conversion rates or expand your keyword reach. Continuously setting new benchmarks keeps your SEO strategy dynamic and aligned with your business objectives.

9. Communicate Results and Adjustments: If you're working with a team or stakeholders, regularly communicate your SEO performance, insights, and any planned adjustments. Keeping everyone informed ensures that your SEO efforts are aligned with broader business goals and that any necessary support or resources are readily available.

10. Be Patient and Persistent: SEO is a long-term strategy that requires ongoing effort and patience. It can take time to see significant results, especially if you're in a competitive industry. Stay persistent, continue to monitor your data, and be willing to make adjustments as needed. Over time, your consistent efforts will pay off with improved rankings, traffic, and business growth.

Tracking your SEO performance is crucial for understanding how well your efforts are working and where you need to make improvements. By monitoring key metrics, setting up regular SEO reports, analyzing traffic, conversions, and ROI, and adjusting your strategy based on data, you can create a dynamic SEO plan that drives continuous growth and success.

SEO is not a set-it-and-forget-it task; it requires constant attention and refinement. By staying data-driven and responsive to what your metrics are telling you, you can make informed decisions that keep your SEO strategy on track and aligned with your business goals. Remember, the ultimate goal of SEO is not just to increase traffic but to attract the right visitors who are more likely to become loyal clients or customers. By focusing on the metrics that matter most and using data to guide your decisions, you can achieve sustainable success in your SEO efforts and grow your accounting business in the digital landscape.

Common SEO Mistakes to Avoid

SEO (Search Engine Optimization for improving your website's visibility and attracting the right audience. However, there are common mistakes that can undermine your efforts and negatively impact your rankings. In this chapter, we will explore some of the most common SEO mistakes to avoid, including over-optimizing your content, ignoring mobile optimization, not keeping up with algorithm changes, and how to correct SEO errors. Understanding these pitfalls and knowing how to fix them will help you maintain a healthy and effective SEO strategy.

Over-Optimizing Your Content

Over-optimizing your content, often referred to as "keyword stuffing," is when you excessively use keywords in your content in an attempt to manipulate search engine rankings. While it might seem like a good idea to include your target keywords as much as possible, over-optimization can actually hurt your SEO rather than help it.

1. What is Over-Optimization?
   - Over-optimization occurs when content is unnaturally loaded with keywords, links, or other SEO elements, making it difficult to read and less useful to the reader. This practice was common in the early days of SEO but is now penalized by search engines like Google.

2. Examples of Over-Optimization:

- Keyword Stuffing: Repeating the same keywords multiple times within your content, meta tags, or alt texts.

- Exact Match Anchor Text: Using the exact same keyword or phrase as anchor text in an excessive number of links.

- Content Cloaking: Presenting different content to search engines and users, often by hiding excessive keywords or links within the code of a page.

3. Why Over-Optimization is Harmful:

- Search engines prioritize user experience and content quality. Over-optimization can make content feel forced, unnatural, and unhelpful to readers, leading to higher bounce rates and lower engagement.

- Search engines like Google have algorithms designed to detect and penalize over-optimized content, which can lead to drops in rankings or even removal from search results.

4. How to Avoid Over-Optimization:

- Focus on Natural Language: Write content that flows naturally and prioritizes readability. Use keywords where they make sense but don't force them into your content.

- Use Synonyms and Related Terms: Instead of repeating the same keyword, use synonyms and related terms that provide context and variation to your content.

- Optimize for User Intent: Consider what your audience is looking for and tailor your content to meet their needs. Providing valuable and relevant information is more important than hitting a specific keyword density.

5. Balancing Optimization:

- Use your main keyword in key areas such as the title, introduction, headings, and a few times naturally throughout the content.

- Include secondary keywords or phrases that are relevant to the topic, but don't overdo it. Focus on content quality and user experience first.

Avoiding over-optimization ensures that your content remains valuable, engaging, and trustworthy, both for your readers and search engines.

Ignoring Mobile Optimization

With the increasing use of smartphones and tablets, mobile optimization is no longer optional—it's a necessity. Ignoring mobile optimization can lead to poor user experience, lower engagement, and a significant drop in search engine rankings, as Google uses mobile-first indexing, which means it primarily uses the mobile version of a website for ranking and indexing.

1. Why Mobile Optimization Matters:
   - Mobile-First Indexing: Google's shift to mobile-first indexing means that the mobile version of your site is considered the primary version. If your site isn't optimized for mobile, it may not perform well in search rankings.
   - User Experience: Mobile users expect fast-loading, easy-to-navigate websites. If your site isn't optimized for mobile, visitors are likely to leave quickly, resulting in high bounce rates.
   - Increasing Mobile Traffic: A significant portion of internet traffic comes from mobile devices. Ignoring mobile optimization means missing out on potential visitors and clients who prefer browsing on their phones or tablets.

2. Common Mobile Optimization Mistakes:
   - Non-Responsive Design: A non-responsive website doesn't adapt well to different screen sizes, making it difficult for mobile users to view and navigate.
   - Slow Load Times: Mobile users expect pages to load quickly. Heavy images, excessive scripts, and poor server performance can slow down your site on mobile devices.
   - Pop-Ups and Interstitial: Pop-ups that are difficult to close or cover the entire screen can frustrate mobile users and lead to penalties from Google.

3. How to Optimize for Mobile:
   - Use Responsive Design: Ensure your website uses a responsive design

that automatically adjusts to fit different screen sizes. This approach provides a consistent user experience across all devices.

- Improve Load Speed: Optimize images, minify CSS and JavaScript, and leverage browser caching to reduce load times on mobile. Tools like Google Page Speed Insights can help you identify and fix speed issues.

- Simplify Navigation: Make navigation easy on mobile by using clear, clickable buttons, minimizing drop down menus, and ensuring that links are easily trappable without zooming in.

4. Testing and Monitoring Mobile Performance:
- Regularly test your website on various mobile devices to ensure it performs well. Use tools like Google's Mobile-Friendly Test and Google Search Console to check for mobile usability issues and address them promptly.

Optimizing your website for mobile ensures that you provide a positive experience for all users, regardless of their device, and helps you maintain or improve your search engine rankings.

Not Keeping Up with Algorithm Changes

Search engine algorithms are constantly evolving, and staying updated with these changes is crucial for maintaining your website's performance in search results. Failing to keep up with algorithm updates can lead to unexpected drops in rankings and traffic, making it harder for your audience to find your content.

1. Why Algorithm Changes Matter:
- Search engines like Google regularly update their algorithms to improve the quality of search results and adapt to changing user behavior. These updates can range from minor tweaks to major changes that significantly impact rankings.

- Algorithm updates often target specific issues, such as content quality, page speed, mobile usability, or back link quality. Websites that fail to meet the new criteria may see a decline in rankings.

2. Common Algorithm Changes to Watch For:
   - Core Updates: These are broad changes to Google's search algorithm that can affect how pages are ranked across all types of queries.
   - Panda Update: Focuses on content quality, penalizing sites with thin, duplicate, or low-quality content.
   - Penguin Update: Targets spammy or manipulative link-building practices, penalizing sites with unnatural back link profiles.
   - Mobile-Friendly Update: Prioritizes sites that are optimized for mobile devices in search results.

3. How to Keep Up with Algorithm Changes:
   - Follow Industry News: Stay informed by following SEO blogs, forums, and news sites like Search Engine Journal, Moz, and Search Engine Land. These sources provide updates on the latest algorithm changes and advice on how to adapt.
   - Monitor Your Site's Performance: Use tools like Google Analytics and Google Search Console to keep an eye on your site's performance. Sudden drops in traffic or rankings can indicate that an algorithm change has affected your site.
   - Adapt Quickly: When a new algorithm update is announced, review the changes and make necessary adjustments to your site. For example, if an update focuses on content quality, consider auditing and improving your existing content.

4. Regular SEO Audits:
   - Conduct regular SEO audits to identify potential issues and areas for improvement. Audits can help you stay proactive and make adjustments before algorithm changes have a negative impact on your site.

Keeping up with algorithm changes and adapting your strategy accordingly helps you maintain a strong SEO presence and avoid penalties that could harm your rankings.

How to Correct SEO Errors

SEO errors can happen to anyone, but the key is to identify and correct them as quickly as possible. Here's a guide on how to correct common SEO errors and get your strategy back on track:

1. Conduct an SEO Audit:
   - An SEO audit is the first step in identifying errors on your website. Use tools like Screaming Frog, Ahrefs, SEMrush, or Google Search Console to perform a comprehensive audit. Look for issues such as broken links, missing meta tags, duplicate content, slow load times, and mobile usability problems.

2. Prioritize Issues:
   - Not all SEO errors are equal in terms of their impact on your site's performance. Prioritize fixing errors that have the most significant effect, such as broken links, missing or duplicate meta tags, and slow page load times. Address critical issues first to see the quickest improvements in your site's performance.

3. Fix Broken Links and Redirects:
   - Broken links can frustrate users and negatively impact your SEO. Use tools like Ahrefs or Screaming Frog to find broken links and set up proper redirects (301 redirects) to guide users and search engines to the correct pages. Avoid using too many redirects in a chain, as this can slow down your site.

4. Optimize Page Load Speed:
   - Slow page load times can lead to higher bounce rates and lower search rankings. Optimize images, minify CSS and JavaScript, enable browser caching, and consider using a Content Delivery Network (CDN) to speed up your site. Regularly test your site's speed with tools like Google Page Speed

Insights and make adjustments as needed.

5. Resolve Duplicate Content Issues:
   - Duplicate content can confuse search engines and dilute the authority of your pages. Use canonical tags to indicate the preferred version of a page when duplicate content is necessary. Remove or consolidate redundant content to ensure that each page on your site offers unique value.

6. Improve Content Quality:
   Improving content quality is essential for meeting user expectations and aligning with search engine guidelines. Review your content to ensure it is informative, well-written, and relevant to your audience. Update outdated information, expand on topics that need more depth, and add visuals like images or videos to make your content more engaging.

7. Optimize for Keywords Naturally:
   - Avoid keyword stuffing and focus on natural keyword placement. Ensure that your primary keywords appear in strategic places like titles, headings, and the first paragraph, but also use variations and related terms throughout the content. Make sure that the use of keywords feels organic and enhances the readability of the content.

8. Fix On-Page SEO Elements:
   - On-page SEO elements, such as meta tags, headers, and alt text for images are crucial for helping search engines understand your content. Ensure that every page has a unique meta title and description, use headers (H1, H2, H3) to structure your content, and add descriptive alt text to all images. This helps improve your visibility and user experience.

9. Enhance Mobile Usability:
   - If your site isn't optimized for mobile, you're missing out on a significant portion of potential traffic. Implement responsive design, improve page load times on mobile, and make navigation simple and user-friendly. Use Google's

Mobile-Friendly Test to identify and fix any mobile usability issues.

10. Regularly Monitor Your Site's Health:
 - SEO is not a one-time task; it requires ongoing monitoring and adjustments. Regularly check your site's health using tools like Google Search Console, which alerts you to crawl errors, security issues, and other problems that could affect your performance. Set up regular site audits to catch and fix issues early.

11. Stay Informed and Adapt:
 - SEO is constantly evolving, so it's important to stay informed about the latest trends and best practices. Attend SEO webinars, read industry blogs, and participate in forums to keep your knowledge up-to-date. Be ready to adapt your strategy in response to new algorithm changes or shifts in user behavior.

12. Seek Professional Help When Needed:
 - Some SEO errors can be complex and may require expert intervention. If you're struggling to fix certain issues or if your rankings have taken a significant hit, consider consulting with an SEO professional or agency. They can provide advanced insights and strategies to help get your SEO back on track.

Avoiding common SEO mistakes is crucial for maintaining a strong online presence and achieving your business goals. By being mindful of over-optimization, prioritizing mobile usability, staying current with algorithm changes, and proactively correcting SEO errors, you can build a robust and effective SEO strategy.

Remember, the key to successful SEO is not just about making your site visible to search engines, but also about providing valuable and relevant content that meets the needs of your audience. By focusing on quality, keeping up with best practices, and continuously monitoring your performance, you can avoid common pitfalls and drive sustainable growth for your website.

SEO is a long-term investment that requires patience, consistency, and adaptability. By avoiding these common mistakes and applying the corrective measures outlined in this chapter, you can enhance your website's performance, attract more targeted traffic, and ultimately achieve better results for your business. Stay committed to learning and improving, and your efforts will pay off in the competitive world of search engine optimization.

Advanced SEO Tactics for Accountants

As the digital landscape evolves, staying ahead of the curve with advanced SEO tactics is crucial for accountants looking to maintain a competitive edge. While basic SEO practices like keyword optimization, back link building, and mobile optimization form the foundation, advanced strategies can significantly enhance your online presence and drive more qualified leads to your business. In this chapter, we will explore advanced SEO tactics for accountants, including content marketing integration, adapting to voice search, understanding E-A-T (Expertise, Authority, Trustworthiness), and preparing for future SEO trends.

Content Marketing Integration

Content marketing is an essential component of a successful SEO strategy. For accountants, integrating content marketing with SEO not only boosts visibility but also establishes your firm as an authority in the industry. Content marketing involves creating and sharing valuable, relevant content that attracts, engages, and retains your target audience.

1. Why Content Marketing Matters for Accountants:
   - Builds Trust and Authority: By providing informative and valuable content, you establish yourself as an expert in the field, building trust with potential clients.
   - Attracts Quality Traffic: Content that addresses specific accounting questions or pain points attracts targeted traffic, increasing the chances of

converting visitors into clients.
- Enhances SEO Performance: High-quality content naturally attracts back links, improves dwell time, and reduces bounce rates, all of which contribute to better SEO performance.

2. Types of Content for Accountants:
- Blog Posts: Regularly publishing blog posts on topics relevant to your audience, such as tax tips, financial planning, and accounting best practices, helps drive organic traffic and engage readers.
- White papers and E-books: In-depth content like white papers and e-books can provide valuable insights and serve as lead magnets to capture email addresses for future marketing efforts.
- Webinars and Videos: Video content, including webinars, tutorials, and client testimonials, can enhance engagement and provide value in a more dynamic format.
- Info graphics: Info graphics simplify complex accounting concepts and data, making them more accessible and shareable on social media and other platforms.

3. Content Marketing Integration with SEO:
- Keyword Research: Before creating content, conduct thorough keyword research to identify the terms and phrases your target audience is searching for. Use these keywords strategically in your content to improve visibility in search results.
- Content Optimization: Optimize each piece of content with relevant keywords, meta tags, headers, and internal links. Ensure that the content is well-structured, easy to read, and provides clear value to the reader.
- Content Distribution: Share your content across multiple channels, including social media, email newsletters, and industry forums. The more visibility your content receives, the more opportunities there are for back links and increased traffic.

4. Measuring Content Performance:

- Use tools like Google Analytics and Google Search Console to track the performance of your content. Monitor metrics such as organic traffic, bounce rate, time on page, and conversion rates to gauge the effectiveness of your content marketing efforts.

Integrating content marketing with your SEO strategy helps you build a robust online presence, attract high-quality leads, and establish your accounting firm as a trusted authority in the industry.

Voice Search and Its Impact on SEO

Voice search is rapidly transforming the way people search for information online. With the increasing use of digital assistants like Siri, Google Assistant, and Alexa, optimizing for voice search has become a crucial aspect of modern SEO. For accountants, adapting to voice search can provide a significant advantage in reaching potential clients who prefer hands-free, conversational searches.

1. Understanding Voice Search:
    - Voice search allows users to speak their queries instead of typing them into a search engine. Voice queries tend to be longer, more conversational, and often framed as questions. For example, instead of typing "tax accountant near me," a user might ask, "Who is the best tax accountant near me?"
    - Voice search is commonly used on mobile devices and smart speakers, making it essential for local SEO and mobile optimization.

2. Why Voice Search Matters for Accountants:
    - Increased Usage: The use of voice search is growing rapidly, with a significant portion of searches now conducted via voice. By optimizing for voice search, you can tap into this expanding audience.
    - Local Searches: Voice searches often have local intent, such as finding nearby services. Optimizing for voice search helps ensure your accounting firm appears in local search results.

- Improved User Experience: Voice search provides quick, hands-free answers, enhancing the user experience and catering to the growing demand for convenience.

3. Optimizing for Voice Search:
    - Focus on Long-Tail Keywords and Questions: Voice searches are typically longer and more conversational. Optimize your content with long-tail keywords and natural language that reflect how people speak. Incorporate questions that users are likely to ask, such as "How can I reduce my tax liability?" or "What are the best accounting tips for small businesses?"
    - Create FAQ Pages: FAQ pages are ideal for voice search optimization because they directly address common questions. Structure your FAQ pages with clear, concise answers to anticipated questions, and include relevant keywords.
    - Improve Page Speed and Mobile Optimization: Voice search users often seek quick answers, so page speed is crucial. Optimize your site's load time and ensure it is mobile-friendly to accommodate voice search users on the go.
    - Claim and Optimize Your Google My Business Listing: Many voice searches have local intent, so make sure your Google My Business profile is up-to-date and optimized. Include accurate contact information, business hours, and relevant keywords in your listing.

4. Structured Data Markup:
    - Implement structured data (schema markup) to help search engines better understand your content and provide more relevant answers to voice search queries. For example, use schema to highlight services, reviews, and FAQs, which can increase your chances of being featured in voice search results.

By optimizing for voice search, you can position your accounting firm to capture a growing segment of search traffic and provide a better user experience for potential clients.

Understanding E-A-T (Expertise, Authority, Trustworthiness)

E-A-T, which stands for Expertise, Authority, and Trustworthiness, is a concept emphasized by Google as a critical factor in evaluating the quality of content on websites. For accountants, demonstrating E-A-T is particularly important because financial advice and accounting services fall under the category of "Your Money or Your Life" (YMYL) topics, which are subject to higher scrutiny by search engines.

1. What is E-A-T?
   - Expertise: Demonstrates that the content is created by someone with the necessary knowledge and qualifications. For accountants, this means showcasing your credentials, certifications, and experience in the field.
   - Authority: Establishes that the content creator or website is recognized as a leading source of information in the industry. This can be built through high-quality back links, mentions from reputable sites, and engagement with industry communities.
   - Trustworthiness: Ensures that your content is reliable, accurate, and secure. Trustworthiness can be enhanced by transparent business practices, clear privacy policies, and positive reviews or testimonials.

2. Why E-A-T Matters for Accountants:
   - Google places a strong emphasis on E-A-T, especially for YMYL topics like accounting, where inaccurate information can have significant financial consequences for users.
   - Demonstrating E-A-T can improve your site's credibility, boost your rankings in search results, and build trust with potential clients who are seeking reliable accounting services.

3. How to Enhance E-A-T on Your Website:
   - Showcase Your Credentials: Include your professional qualifications, certifications, and memberships in recognized accounting bodies on your website. Highlight your team's expertise and any notable achievements or

awards.

- Create Authoritative Content: Publish in-depth articles, guides, and resources that demonstrate your knowledge and expertise in accounting. Back up your claims with data, case studies, and references from reputable sources.

- Build High-Quality Back links: Focus on earning back links from reputable and authoritative websites, such as industry publications, educational institutions, and respected blogs. Quality back links signal to search engines that your content is valuable and trustworthy.

- Encourage Reviews and Testimonials: Positive reviews and testimonials from satisfied clients can significantly enhance your site's trustworthiness. Display these reviews prominently on your website and on third-party platforms like Google My Business.

4. Maintain Transparency and Accuracy:

- Ensure that your content is up-to-date, accurate, and free of errors. Provide clear information about your services, pricing, and contact details. Use secure protocols (HTTPS) to protect user data and build trust with your audience.

By focusing on E-A-T, you can strengthen your online reputation, improve your SEO performance, and attract more qualified leads to your accounting firm.

Preparing for Future SEO Trends

The world of SEO is constantly evolving, with new technologies and trends emerging that can impact how businesses connect with their audience. To stay ahead, accountants need to be proactive in preparing for future SEO trends. Here are some key trends to watch and how you can prepare for them:

1. Artificial Intelligence and Machine Learning:
    - Search engines are increasingly using AI and machine learning to

better understand search intent and deliver more relevant results. Google's AI-driven algorithm, Rank Brain, continues to play a significant role in determining search rankings.

- Preparation: Focus on creating high-quality, user-eccentric content that aligns with search intent. Use AI-powered tools like Clear scope or Market Muse to optimize content for relevance and comprehensiveness.

2. The Rise of Video Content:

- Video content is becoming more popular, with platforms like YouTube, Ticktock, and Instagram driving massive engagement. Video can be a powerful tool for explaining complex accounting concepts and connecting with a broader audience.

- Preparation: Incorporate video
content into your SEO strategy by creating informative videos on topics like tax tips, financial planning, or step-by-step guides for small businesses. Optimize your videos with relevant keywords, clear titles, and detailed descriptions, and consider embedding videos on your website to enhance user engagement and time on site.

3. Emphasis on User Experience (UX):

- Google's Core Web Vitals update emphasizes the importance of user experience, including page load speed, interactivity, and visual stability. Websites that provide a better UX are likely to rank higher in search results.

- Preparation: Regularly audit your website's performance using tools like Google Page Speed Insights and Lighthouse. Focus on improving load times, minimizing layout shifts, and ensuring that your site is easy to navigate on both desktop and mobile devices.

4. Increased Importance of Local SEO:

- As more users search for services near them, local SEO continues to grow in importance. Google's algorithms are placing more emphasis on proximity, relevance, and prominence for local search results.

- Preparation: Keep your Google My Business profile up-to-date, encourage local reviews, and optimize your content for location-specific keywords. Ensure your name, address, and phone number (NAP) are consistent across all online directories.

5. Voice Search Optimization:
   - With the rise of smart speakers and voice-activated assistants, voice search is expected to continue growing. Voice searches tend to be longer and more conversational, often framed as questions.
   - Preparation: Optimize your content for natural language and question-based queries. Create content that answers common questions in a concise, straightforward manner, and consider implementing structured data to help search engines better understand your content.

6. Greater Focus on Data Privacy and Security:
   - Data privacy concerns are leading to stricter regulations and an increased focus on user data protection. Websites that fail to prioritize security may suffer in search rankings.
   - Preparation: Ensure your website uses HTTPS, has a clear privacy policy, and follows best practices for data protection. Be transparent about how you collect, use, and protect user data to build trust with your audience.

7. Structured Data and Rich Snippets:
   - Structured data helps search engines understand the content of your pages, which can lead to enhanced search results like rich snippets. Rich snippets provide additional information directly in search results, such as ratings, prices, or FAQs, which can improve your click-through rate.
   - Preparation: Implement structured data markup on your website to make your content more accessible to search engines. Use schema.org to add markup for articles, services, reviews, and FAQs, and test your implementation using Google's Structured Data Testing Tool.

8. Sustainability and Ethical Practices:
   - As environmental awareness grows, businesses are expected to demon-

strate sustainable and ethical practices. Consumers and search engines alike are increasingly favoring brands that reflect responsible values.

- Preparation: Highlight your firm's commitment to sustainability, community involvement, and ethical practices on your website. This not only appeals to conscientious consumers but also enhances your brand image and trustworthiness.

9. Adapting to Zero-Click Searches:
- Zero-click searches occur when users find the information they need directly on the search results page, often through featured snippets, knowledge panels, or other SERP features. This trend reduces the need for users to click through to websites.
- Preparation: Aim to capture featured snippets by answering common questions clearly and concisely in your content. Use headers, bullet points, and structured data to increase your chances of being featured in zero-click search results.

10. Continued Rise of Artificial Intelligence and Automation in SEO:
- AI and automation tools are becoming more prevalent in SEO, helping marketers with tasks like content optimization, keyword research, and competitive analysis. These tools can save time and provide deeper insights into SEO performance.

- Preparation: Explore AI-powered SEO tools that can help streamline your processes and provide data-driven recommendations. Stay informed about the latest advancements in AI for SEO to leverage these technologies effectively

Advanced SEO tactics are essential for accountants looking to stay ahead in an increasingly competitive digital landscape. By integrating content marketing with SEO, adapting to the rise of voice search, emphasizing E-A-T principles, and preparing for future SEO trends, you can build a robust online presence that attracts and retains clients.

As SEO continues to evolve, it's crucial to remain adaptable and proactive in your approach. Regularly update your knowledge, invest in the right tools, and be willing to experiment with new strategies. By doing so, you can ensure that your accounting firm not only keeps up with the latest SEO developments but also thrives in the ever-changing digital world.

Staying ahead of SEO trends means continuously learning and refining your tactics. Focus on creating value-driven content, improving user experience, and demonstrating your expertise, authority, and trustworthiness. By preparing for the future of SEO, you position your accounting firm for long-term success, connecting with more potential clients and establishing yourself as a leader in the field.

SEO Case Studies and Success Stories

Learning from real-world examples is one of the best ways to understand the impact of SEO on accounting firms. By examining case studies and success stories, we can see how targeted strategies can significantly improve visibility, traffic, and client acquisition. In this chapter, we will explore several case studies of SEO in accounting, highlight lessons learned from successful campaigns, and illustrate how even small changes can lead to big results.

Real-World Examples of SEO in Accounting

SEO can transform the online presence of accounting firms, making it easier for potential clients to find them in search results. Below, we discuss real-world examples of how accounting firms have used SEO to achieve impressive outcomes.

1. Case Study 1: Boosting Local Visibility for a Small Accounting Firm

- Background: A small accounting firm in a mid-sized city struggled to attract local clients due to a lack of online presence. Despite offering excellent services, they were not ranking well in local search results for terms like "tax accountant near me" or "small business accountant in [City]."

- SEO Strategy: The firm partnered with an SEO agency to improve their local visibility. The strategy included optimizing their Google My Business profile, creating location-specific landing pages, and acquiring local citations from relevant directories.

- Actions Taken:
  - Google My Business Optimization: The firm's Google My Business profile was updated with accurate information, including business hours, services offered, and high-quality images. Regular posts and updates were added to keep the profile active and engaging.
  - Local Content Creation: The firm created blog posts targeting local keywords, such as "best accounting tips for small businesses in [City]." They also added client testimonials with a local focus to build trust with potential clients.
  - Building Local Citations: The firm's NAP (Name, Address, Phone Number) was made consistent across various local directories and business listings. This helped reinforce their local presence in search engines.

- Results: Within six months, the firm's visibility in local search results improved significantly. They started appearing in the top three positions of the Google Local Pack for relevant searches, resulting in a 50% increase in website traffic and a 40% increase in local inquiries. The firm's client base grew, and they reported a 30% increase in new client acquisition from local searches alone.

- Key Takeaway: Local SEO is a powerful tool for small accounting firms to attract nearby clients. By optimizing local listings, creating relevant content, and maintaining a consistent online presence, firms can greatly enhance their visibility and attract more business.

2. Case Study 2: Leveraging Content Marketing to Drive Traffic

- Background: A mid-sized accounting firm specializing in tax services wanted to increase its organic traffic and establish itself as a thought leader in the industry. Despite having a modern website, their blog was underutilized, and they had limited content that addressed client concerns.

- SEO Strategy: The firm launched a comprehensive content marketing campaign focused on providing valuable information to their target audience. The campaign included creating in-depth blog posts, guides, and case studies that addressed common tax-related questions and concerns.

- Actions Taken:
   - Keyword Research and Content Planning: Extensive keyword research was conducted to identify popular search terms and questions related to tax services. A content calendar was developed to ensure regular publication of blog posts and guides.
   - High-Quality Content Creation: The firm produced detailed articles on topics such as "Tax Deductions for Freelancers," "How to Prepare for an IRS Audit," and "Common Tax Filing Mistakes to Avoid." Each piece was optimized for SEO with targeted keywords, meta tags, and internal links.
   - Promoting Content: The firm promoted their content through social media, email newsletters, and by reaching out to industry influences who shared their articles.

- Results: Over a 12-month period, the firm's organic traffic increased by 150%. Their blog became a top source of traffic, accounting for nearly 60% of all website visits. The firm also received numerous back links from reputable websites, further boosting their SEO performance. Most importantly, they saw a 25% increase in leads generated from their website, as more visitors were converting into inquiries and consultations.

- Key Takeaway: Content marketing is highly effective for accountants looking to build authority and drive organic traffic. By creating valuable, informative content that addresses client pain points, firms can attract more visitors, enhance their reputation, and generate more leads.

3. Case Study 3: Improving User Experience to Boost Conversions

- Background: A large accounting firm noticed that while they were receiving a good amount of traffic, their conversion rate was lower than expected. Visitors were not filling out contact forms or scheduling consultations at the desired rate, indicating potential issues with the website's user experience (UX).

- SEO Strategy: The firm decided to focus on improving the UX of their website to encourage more visitors to take action. This included optimizing page load times, simplifying navigation, and enhancing the overall design to make the site more user-friendly.

- Actions Taken:
    - Page Speed Optimization: The firm used tools like Google Page Speed Insights to identify and fix elements that were slowing down their site, such as large images and unused JavaScript. They implemented a Content Delivery Network (CDN) and improved server response times.

- Improving Navigation and Design: The website's navigation was streamlined to make it easier for users to find key information. Call-to-action buttons were made more prominent, and the design was updated to be clean and professional.

- A/B Testing: The firm conducted A/B testing on landing pages to determine which layouts, headlines, and calls-to-action were most effective at converting visitors into leads.

- Results: The improvements led to a 30% reduction in bounce rate and a 20% increase in average session duration. Most importantly, the firm's conversion rate increased by 35%, resulting in a significant boost in consultations and new client sign-ups.

- Key Takeaway: User experience is a critical component of SEO that directly affects conversions. By making your website faster, easier to navigate, and more appealing to visitors, you can significantly increase the likelihood of turning traffic into paying clients.

Lessons Learned from Successful SEO Campaigns

The above case studies highlight several important lessons for accountants looking to succeed with SEO:

1. Local SEO is Essential: For accounting firms that rely on local clients, optimizing for local search is crucial. This includes maintaining a well-optimized Google My Business profile, creating local content, and ensuring consistency across local citations.

2. Content is King: High-quality, informative content that addresses the needs and concerns of your target audience can drive significant traffic and build authority. Regularly publishing valuable content not only attracts visitors but also encourages them to stay and engage with your website.

3. User Experience Matters: A well-designed, fast-loading website that offers a great user experience can greatly enhance your SEO efforts. By focusing on UX, you can reduce bounce rates, increase time on site, and improve conversion rates.

4. SEO is an Ongoing Process: Successful SEO campaigns require continuous effort, monitoring, and adaptation. The digital landscape and search engine algorithms are constantly changing, so staying proactive and flexible is key to maintaining your rankings and visibility.

5. Data-Driven Decisions Lead to Success: Use data and analytics to guide your SEO strategy. Regularly track your performance, test different approaches, and make adjustments based on what the data tells you. A data-driven approach helps you focus on what works and avoid wasting resources on ineffective tactics.

SEO CASE STUDIES AND SUCCESS STORIES

How Small Changes Can Lead to Big Results

In many cases, small, targeted changes can have a significant impact on SEO performance. Here are some examples of small changes that led to big results for accounting firms:

1. Optimizing Meta Tags: A small firm noticed that their click-through rate (CTR) from search results was lower than expected. By revising their meta titles and descriptions to be more engaging and accurately reflect the content, they saw a 20% increase in CTR within a month. This simple change helped drive more traffic to their site without altering their rankings.

2. Improving Internal Linking: An accounting firm improved its internal linking structure by adding relevant links between related blog posts and service pages. This not only helped users navigate the site more easily but also boosted the SEO value of linked pages. As a result, the firm saw a 15% increase in page views and a slight improvement in their rankings for key service-related keywords.

3. Updating Outdated Content: A mid-sized accounting firm reviewed its blog and identified several outdated posts that were no longer relevant By updating the content with current information, adding new insights, and optimizing for relevant keywords, they revived the performance of these posts. This led to a 25% increase in organic traffic to their blog, demonstrating the power of keeping content fresh and up-to-date.

4. Enhancing Mobile Usability: A firm realized that a significant portion of their traffic was coming from mobile devices, but their site wasn't fully optimized for mobile users. By making simple adjustments such as increasing font size, optimizing images, and improving mobile navigation, they enhanced the user experience for mobile visitors. This resulted in a 30% reduction in bounce rate for mobile users and an overall increase in engagement.

5. Adding Structured Data: An accounting firm added structured data (schema markup) to their website to help search engines better understand their content. This small change improved their chances of appearing in rich snippets, which can increase visibility in search results. Within a few months, the firm saw an increase in traffic from featured snippets, driving more qualified leads to their site.

6. Utilizing Customer Reviews: A firm noticed that they had a handful of positive customer reviews that were not being highlighted effectively. By adding a dedicated testimonials page and integrating customer reviews prominently on their service pages, the firm was able to showcase their credibility and build trust with potential clients. This simple change led to a 20% increase in lead inquiries, as prospective clients felt more confident in the firm's capabilities after reading positive feedback from others.

Lessons from Small Changes Leading to Big Results

These examples illustrate that you don't always need to undertake large, complex projects to see significant improvements in your SEO performance. Sometimes, small, strategic adjustments can make a substantial difference. Here are key takeaways on how small changes can lead to big results:

1. Focus on User Intent: Enhancing meta tags, updating outdated content, or improving internal linking are all actions that align better with user intent. By making small tweaks to meet what users are looking for, you can significantly boost engagement and satisfaction.

2. Consistency is Key: Consistency in your SEO efforts, whether it's regularly updating content, optimizing for mobile, or adding new internal links, helps maintain and gradually improve your site's performance over time. Regular maintenance and small adjustments prevent issues from compounding and allow you to stay competitive.

3. Monitor and Adapt: Continuously monitor your site's performance using tools like Google Analytics and Google Search Console. When you identify areas that are under performing, even minor optimizations can lead to meaningful improvements. Being responsive to your data keeps your SEO strategy agile and effective.

4. Leverage Customer Feedback: Highlighting customer reviews and testimonials is a quick win that can enhance trust and credibility. Don't underestimate the impact that social proof can have on your conversion rates.

5. Keep Content Fresh and Relevant: SEO is not a one-time task; it requires ongoing attention. Regularly revisiting your content to ensure it's current, relevant, and optimized for search can breathe new life into pages that have fallen behind.

6. Enhance Mobile Experience: With a growing number of users accessing websites on mobile devices, improving mobile usability should be a top priority. Simple changes to make your site more mobile-friendly can lead to lower bounce rates and higher user satisfaction, directly impacting your SEO performance.

7. Structured Data Implementation: Adding structured data is a relatively small technical adjustment that can have outsizes benefits, such as increasing your visibility in rich snippets and enhancing your click-through rates from search results.

Real-world examples and case studies of SEO success in accounting show the transformative power of targeted SEO strategies. From boosting local visibility and leveraging content marketing to enhancing user experience and making small but impactful adjustments, these stories highlight the tangible benefits of investing in SEO.

For accountants, the lessons learned from these successful campaigns underscore the importance of a holistic approach to SEO. This involves not only optimizing for keywords and back links but also focusing on user experience, content quality, and adaptability to changing trends and technologies.

Small changes, when strategically implemented, can yield significant results, proving that SEO is about consistent, ongoing improvement rather than just large, sweeping overhauls. By paying attention to the details and being responsive to data, accounting firms can achieve sustained growth, attract more clients, and build lasting authority in their field.

Ultimately, the key to successful SEO is understanding that it is an evolving process that requires dedication, experimentation, and a willingness to learn from both successes and challenges. By continually refining your approach and staying informed about best practices and new opportunities, you can keep your accounting firm at the forefront of the digital landscape and achieve long-term success in attracting and retaining clients.

Developing an Ongoing SEO Strategy

SEO (Search Engine Optimization) is not a one-time task but a continuous process that requires consistent effort, regular updates, and strategic planning to achieve long-term success. For accountants, developing an ongoing SEO strategy is crucial for maintaining visibility, attracting new clients, and staying competitive in an ever-evolving digital landscape. In this chapter, we will explore how to plan for long-term SEO success, perform regular SEO maintenance, scale your SEO efforts as your practice grows, and set future SEO goals.

Planning for Long-Term SEO Success

A successful long-term SEO strategy begins with careful planning and a clear understanding of your business goals. By aligning your SEO efforts with your overall business objectives, you can create a road map that guides your actions and ensures sustained growth.

1. Define Your SEO Objectives:
   - Start by identifying what you want to achieve with your SEO efforts. Common objectives for accountants might include increasing website traffic, generating more leads, improving local search visibility, or establishing your firm as a thought leader in the accounting industry.
   - Make sure your objectives are specific, measurable, achievable, relevant, and time-bound (SMART). For example, instead of simply aiming to "increase traffic," set a goal to "increase organic traffic by 30% within the next six

months."

2. Understand Your Target Audience:
 - Clearly define your target audience, including their needs, pain points, and search behaviors. Are you targeting small business owners looking for tax help, individuals seeking financial advice, or large corporations needing complex accounting services?
 - Use tools like Google Analytics, Google Search Console, and customer surveys to gain insights into your audience's demographics, interests, and the keywords they use when searching for accounting services.

3. Conduct a Comprehensive SEO Audit:
 - Before developing your long-term strategy, conduct a comprehensive SEO audit to assess your current performance and identify areas for improvement. An audit should cover on-page SEO (content, meta tags, internal linking), off-page SEO (back links, domain authority), technical SEO (site speed, mobile usability), and local SEO (Google My Business profile, local citations).
 - Use the findings from your audit to prioritize tasks and allocate resources effectively. For example, if your audit reveals that your site has slow load times or lacks mobile optimization, these should be top priorities to address.

4. Create a Content Strategy:
 - Content is a critical component of any long-term SEO plan. Develop a content strategy that aligns with your business goals and addresses the needs of your audience. Plan a mix of blog posts, guides, videos, info graphics, and other content types that provide value and drive traffic.
 - Use keyword research to identify topics that resonate with your target audience and have good search potential. Regularly update your content calendar to ensure a steady stream of fresh, relevant content.

5. Develop a Link-Building Plan:
 - High-quality back links from reputable websites are essential for improving your site's authority and rankings. Develop a link-building plan

DEVELOPING AN ONGOING SEO STRATEGY

that includes guest blogging, creating shareable content, and building relationships with industry influences.

- Focus on acquiring links from relevant, authoritative sites, such as accounting associations, financial blogs, or local business directories. Avoid spammy or low-quality links, as these can harm your SEO efforts.

6. Set Up Analytics and Reporting:
   - Use tools like Google Analytics, Google Search Console, and other SEO software to track your performance. Set up regular reports that monitor key metrics such as organic traffic, keyword rankings, conversion rates, and back links.
   - Regular reporting allows you to measure progress, identify trends, and adjust your strategy as needed. Use data to make informed decisions and keep your SEO efforts aligned with your business objectives.

7. Allocate Resources and Set a Budget:
   - Determine the resources needed to execute your SEO strategy, including time, personnel, and budget. Consider whether you will handle SEO in-house or hire external help, such as an SEO agency or consultants.

- Allocate a budget for necessary tools, content creation, and any outsourced services. A well-defined budget helps ensure that your SEO efforts are sustainable and can scale as your business grows.

By planning carefully and setting clear objectives, you can create a solid foundation for your long-term SEO strategy that supports sustained growth and success.

SEO Maintenance: Regular Checks and Updates

SEO is not a "set it and forget it" task; it requires ongoing maintenance to keep your website optimized and performing well. Regular checks and updates are essential to address issues, adapt to changes in search engine algorithms, and stay ahead of your competition.

1. Regular Site Audits:
   - Conduct regular site audits to ensure your website remains optimized for search engines. This should include checking for broken links, updating meta tags, verifying that pages are indexed correctly, and ensuring that your site remains mobile-friendly and fast-loading.
   - Use tools like Screaming Frog, Ahrefs, or SEMrush to perform these audits efficiently. Aim to conduct a full audit at least once every quarter, with lighter checks more frequently.

2. Content Refresh and Updates:
   - Content that is outdated or no longer relevant can harm your SEO. Regularly review your existing content to ensure it remains current and valuable. Update statistics, refresh old blog posts, and remove or consolidate redundant pages.
   - Consider adding new sections or insights to evergreen content to keep it fresh and relevant. Regular updates signal to search engines that your site is active and continuously providing valuable information.

3. Monitor Keyword Performance:
   - Continuously track the performance of your target keywords. Keywords that were once highly effective may become less so over time as search trends change. Regularly update your keyword strategy to include new terms and phrases that are gaining traction.
   - Use tools like Google Search Console, Ahrefs, and SEMrush to monitor keyword rankings and adjust your content accordingly.

4. Check Back links and Disavow Spammy Links:
   - Regularly monitor your back link profile to ensure that your site is earning high-quality links. Use tools like Ahrefs or Moz to track your back links and identify any spammy or harmful links.
   - If you find low-quality or suspicious links pointing to your site, use

DEVELOPING AN ONGOING SEO STRATEGY

Google's Disavow Tool to disassociate your site from these links. This helps protect your site's authority and prevents penalties from search engines.

5. Update Technical SEO Elements:
   - Regularly check your site's technical health, including page load speeds, mobile usability, and structured data. As search engine algorithms evolve, the importance of these elements may change, so staying current is key.
   - Ensure that your site s architecture remains clean and that search engines can easily crawl and index your pages. Address any technical issues promptly to maintain optimal performance.

6. Stay Informed About Algorithm Updates:
   - Search engine algorithms are constantly evolving, and updates can have a significant impact on your rankings. Stay informed about major updates from Google and other search engines by following SEO news sites, blogs, and forums.
   - When a significant update occurs, assess its impact on your site and make any necessary adjustments to your SEO strategy. Being proactive in responding to algorithm changes helps mitigate potential negative effects.

7. Engage with User Feedback:
   - User feedback, including comments, reviews, and inquiries, can provide valuable insights into how well your site meets visitor needs. Regularly engage with user feedback to identify areas for improvement and to make your site more user-friendly.
   - Incorporating feedback into your SEO strategy not only improves the user experience but also demonstrates to search engines that your site values and responds to its audience.

Regular SEO maintenance ensures that your website remains optimized, relevant, and competitive. By keeping a close eye on your site's performance and making timely updates, you can sustain and build upon your SEO success over time.

Scaling Your SEO Efforts as Your Practice Grows

As your accounting practice grows, so should your SEO efforts. Scaling your SEO strategy involves expanding your reach, targeting new keywords, producing more content, and refining your tactics to support a larger, more diverse audience.

1. Expand Your Content Strategy:
   - As your practice expands, consider broadening your content strategy to cover a wider range of topics and services. For example, if you initially focused on tax advice for individuals, you might expand to include content on corporate accounting, investment planning, or international tax issues.
   - Diversify your content types by incorporating more videos, webinars, podcasts, and interactive tools like calculators or quizzes. This variety can help you reach different segments of your audience and keep them engaged.

2. Target New Keywords and Markets:
   - Scaling your SEO strategy might involve targeting new keywords that reflect the growing scope of your services. Conduct regular keyword research to identify opportunities to reach new markets or cater to specific niches within accounting.
   - Consider expanding your geographic reach if your firm is opening new locations or offering virtual services. Local SEO can be scaled to target multiple locations, helping you attract clients from a broader area.

3. Invest in Advanced SEO Tools:
   - As your practice grows, the complexity of managing your SEO efforts will increase. Invest in advanced SEO tools that offer comprehensive features for keyword tracking, content optimization, back link analysis, and reporting.
   - Tools like Ahrefs, SEMrush, Moz Pro, and others offer enterprise-level features that can help you scale your SEO efforts effectively. Investing in these tools can save time and provide deeper insights into your performance.

DEVELOPING AN ONGOING SEO STRATEGY

4. Consider Outsourcing or Expanding Your SEO Team:
   - Scaling SEO efforts often requires additional expertise and resources. If your in-house team is at capacity, consider outsourcing specific tasks to SEO consultants or agencies that specialize in accounting or professional services.
   - Alternatively, you can expand your internal SEO team by hiring new talent with specialized skills in areas like content marketing, technical SEO, or data analysis.

5. Refine and Automate Processes:
   As your SEO efforts grow, refining and automating processes can help manage the increasing workload more efficiently. Automate routine tasks like reporting, keyword tracking, and site audits using SEO tools and software. Implement workflows that streamline content creation, publication, and distribution to ensure consistency and quality as you scale.

6. Leverage Data and Analytics for Strategic Growth:
   - Use data-driven insights to identify high-performing areas and opportunities for expansion. For example, analyze which types of content generate the most traffic or leads, and focus on scaling those efforts.
   - Segment your audience data to tailor your content and SEO strategies to specific groups, such as small business owners, individual taxpayers, or large corporations. This targeted approach can help you maximize the effectiveness of your scaled efforts.

7. Enhance Local SEO for Multiple Locations:
   - If your practice expands to multiple locations, ensure that your local SEO strategy is adapted to each market. Create individual location pages on your website, optimize them with local keywords, and maintain separate Google My Business profiles for each office.
   - Encourage reviews for each location and ensure that NAP (Name, Address, Phone number) information is consistent across all directories and listings. This strategy will help you capture local searches in each area where you operate.

8. Increase Your Investment in Paid Advertising:
   - As part of scaling your SEO strategy, consider integrating paid search advertising (PPC) to complement your organic efforts. This can be particularly effective for targeting high-value keywords or launching campaigns in new markets.
   - Use paid ads to support SEO during periods of significant algorithm changes or when entering highly competitive niches. Paid campaigns can provide immediate visibility while you work on building long-term organic rankings.

Setting Future SEO Goals

Setting future SEO goals is essential for maintaining momentum and guiding your efforts as your accounting practice continues to grow. Clear, strategic goals will help you focus your resources, measure progress, and adapt to the ever-changing landscape of SEO.

1. Align SEO Goals with Business Objectives:
   - Your SEO goals should be closely aligned with your broader business objectives. For example, if your goal is to expand into a new service area, set specific SEO goals around ranking for relevant keywords, driving traffic to those service pages, and generating leads.
   - Consider the overall growth trajectory of your practice and set goals that reflect your long-term vision. This might include expanding your geographic reach, targeting new client demographics, or increasing your market share in specific accounting niches.

2. Set Incremental and Milestone Goals:
   - Break down your long-term SEO goals into smaller, manageable milestones. For example, if your objective is to double your organic traffic in two years, set incremental goals to increase traffic by 10% each quarter.
   - Milestone goals help you track progress and keep your team motivated. They also allow you to make adjustments along the way if certain strategies

aren't delivering the expected results.

3. Focus on Continuous Improvement:
   - SEO is not static; it requires ongoing effort and refinement. Set goals around continuous improvement, such as increasing the average session duration, reducing bounce rates, or enhancing the quality of your back links.

- Continuously test different strategies and be open to experimenting with new SEO techniques, such as voice search optimization, AI-driven content creation, or new content formats like interactive tools.

4. Plan for Algorithm Changes and Industry Shifts:
   - Given the frequency of search engine algorithm updates, plan for potential impacts on your SEO strategy. Set goals that include building a resilient SEO foundation that can weather these changes, such as maintaining a diverse back link profile and focusing on content quality and user experience.

- Stay adaptable and be prepared to pivot your strategy in response to changes in the accounting industry or shifts in client behavior. Regularly review your goals and adjust them as necessary to stay aligned with the latest trends and opportunities.

5. Measure Success with KPIs and Benchmarks:
   - Use key performance indicators (KPIs) to measure the success of your SEO efforts. Common KPIs for SEO include organic traffic, keyword rankings conversion rates, and ROI.

- Establish benchmarks based on your current performance and industry standards. Use these benchmarks to set realistic goals and track your progress over time. Regularly review and update your KPIs to ensure they remain relevant to your evolving SEO strategy.

6. Set Goals for Team Development and Training:

- As SEO practices evolve, so should the skills and knowledge of your team. Set goals around team development, such as attending SEO workshops, obtaining certifications, or participating in industry conferences.

- Encourage continuous learning and knowledge sharing within your team to keep everyone up-to-date on the latest SEO trends and best practices. A well-trained team is better equipped to adapt to changes and drive your SEO strategy forward.

7. Include Client-Eccentric Goals:
   - SEO success is not just about increasing numbers; it's also about meeting client needs and expectations. Set goals that focus on enhancing the user experience, such as improving site navigation, providing more personalized content, or increasing engagement with interactive elements on your site.

- Consider implementing client feedback loops, such as surveys or feedback forms, to gather insights on how well your SEO efforts are aligning with client expectations. Use this feedback to refine your strategy and set client-focused SEO goals.

8. Review and Adjust Goals Regularly:
   - SEO is dynamic, and so should be your approach to setting goals. Regularly review your progress towards your goals and adjust them as needed based on performance data, market conditions, or changes in your business strategy.

- Schedule quarterly or biannual reviews of your SEO goals to assess what's working and where adjustments are needed. Keeping your goals flexible and adaptable ensures that your SEO strategy remains relevant and effective over time.

Developing an ongoing SEO strategy is essential for accounting firms seeking long-term success in the digital marketplace. By planning for the future, conducting regular maintenance, scaling efforts as your practice grows, and setting clear, strategic goals, you can build a robust SEO framework that supports your business objectives.

SEO is an evolving process that requires dedication, flexibility, and a commitment to continuous improvement. By staying proactive, leveraging data-driven insights, and being willing to adapt to changes in the digital landscape, you can achieve sustained growth and keep your accounting firm at the forefront of search engine results.

As your practice evolves, so too should your SEO strategy. By continuously refining your approach, setting new goals, and scaling your efforts to match the growth of your business, you can ensure that your SEO efforts remain effective and aligned with your long-term vision. With the right strategy in place, your accounting firm can enjoy the benefits of increased visibility, higher client acquisition, and a strong online presence that supports your overall business success.

Conclusion

SEO (Search Engine Optimization) is a powerful tool that can significantly boost the online presence of accounting firms, helping them attract new clients, improve their brand visibility, and establish authority in a competitive market. This chapter will recap the key SEO concepts for beginners, provide guidance on how to continue learning and improving your SEO skills, offer encouragement and practical next steps, and share final tips for achieving SEO success in the accounting industry. By understanding and applying these concepts, you can build a strong foundation for your ongoing SEO efforts and ensure your accounting practice thrives in the digital landscape.

Recap of Key SEO Concepts for Beginners

Throughout this guide, we have covered a broad range of SEO topics that are essential for accounting firms looking to enhance their online visibility. Here is a recap of the key concepts to keep in mind as you continue your SEO journey:

1. Understanding SEO Basics:
    - SEO is the process of optimizing your website to rank higher in search engine results, thereby increasing the quantity and quality of traffic to your site. For accountants, effective SEO means making your services easily discoverable by potential clients searching for accounting help online.

2. Keyword Research:
   - Keywords are the words and phrases that potential clients use when searching for accounting services. Conducting thorough keyword research allows you to identify the terms most relevant to your audience. Focus on a mix of high-value and long-tail keywords that reflect the specific services you offer.

3. On-Page SEO:
   - On-page SEO involves optimizing individual pages on your website to improve their search engine rankings. Key elements include optimizing meta titles and descriptions, using header tags, incorporating keywords naturally into your content, and ensuring your site's structure is user-friendly and accessible.

4. Content Marketing:
   - Content is at the heart of successful SEO. Regularly publishing high-quality, relevant content—such as blog posts, guides, videos, and info graphics—helps you attract and engage your audience. Content marketing not only drives traffic but also establishes your firm as a knowledgeable authority in the accounting industry.

5. Technical SEO:
   - Technical SEO focuses on the backend aspects of your website that affect its performance in search engines. This includes ensuring fast page load times, having a mobile-friendly design, securing your site with HTTPS, and implementing structured data to help search engines understand your content better.

6. Local SEO:
   - For accounting firms that serve specific geographic areas, local SEO is crucial. This involves optimizing your Google My Business profile, earning local citations, and encouraging positive reviews from satisfied clients. Local SEO helps you rank higher for location-specific searches and connect with

clients in your area.

7. Link Building:
- Link building is the process of acquiring back links from other reputable websites. High-quality back links signal to search engines that your site is trustworthy and authoritative. Focus on earning links naturally by creating valuable content that others want to share and link to.

8. User Experience (UX):
- SEO is not just about pleasing search engines; it's also about creating a positive experience for your visitors. A well-designed, easy-to-navigate website that loads quickly and works well on all devices will keep users engaged and encourage them to take action, such as contacting your firm for a consultation.

9. Tracking and Analyzing Performance:
- Regularly monitor your SEO performance using tools like Google Analytics, Google Search Console, and other SEO software. Track key metrics such as organic traffic, keyword rankings, conversion rates, and bounce rates. Use this data to make informed decisions and adjust your strategy as needed.

10. Staying Updated with SEO Trends:
- SEO is a constantly evolving field, with search engine algorithms frequently changing. Stay informed about the latest trends and updates by following SEO blogs, participating in webinars, and engaging with online communities. Continuous learning and adaptation are key to maintaining your SEO success over time.

By mastering these fundamental concepts, you can build a solid foundation for your SEO strategy and position your accounting firm for sustained growth and success.

How to Continue Learning and Improving

CONCLUSION

SEO is a journey of continuous learning and improvement. The digital landscape evolves rapidly, and staying updated with the latest best practices is essential for maintaining your competitive edge. Here are some ways to continue learning and improving your SEO skills:

1. Follow Industry Leaders and Blogs:
   - Keep up with the latest SEO insights and updates by following industry leaders and reputable SEO blogs. Websites like Moz, Search Engine Journal, and Search Engine Land regularly publish articles, case studies, and research that can help you stay informed about changes in SEO practices.

2. Participate in Online Courses and Certifications:
   - Many online platforms offer courses on SEO, ranging from beginner to advanced levels. Websites like Coursera, Udemy, and Hub Spot Academy provide structured learning paths that cover various aspects of SEO. Earning certifications can also enhance your credibility and deepen your knowledge.

3. Join SEO Communities and Forums:
   - Engage with SEO communities on platforms like Reddit (e.g., r/SEO), LinkedIn groups, and SEO-focused forums. These communities provide a space to ask questions, share experiences, and learn from other professionals facing similar challenges.

4. Attend Webinars and Conferences:
   - SEO webinars, workshops, and conferences are excellent opportunities to learn from experts, network with peers, and gain new insights into SEO strategies. Events like MozCon, SMX (Search Marketing Expo), and BrightonSEO feature speakers who are at the forefront of the industry

5. Experiment and Test:
   - SEO is not a one-size-fits-all approach. Regularly experiment with different tactics, test new ideas, and analyze the results. A/B testing your meta descriptions, page layouts, or call-to-action buttons can reveal what

works best for your audience and help you refine your strategy.

6. Use SEO Tools:
  - SEO tools like Ahrefs, SEMrush, Moz Pro, and Google's suite of tools (Analytics, Search Console) are invaluable for tracking performance and identifying areas for improvement. These tools often come with tutorials and resources that can help you learn how to use them effectively.

7. Stay Updated on Algorithm Changes:
  - Search engines, particularly Google, frequently update their algorithms. Stay alert to major updates and understand their impact on search rankings. Following Google's official blogs or subscribing to SEO news alerts can help you stay on top of these changes.

8. Read Case Studies:
  - Case studies provide real-world examples of what works and what doesn't in SEO. By learning from the successes and failures of others, you can avoid common pitfalls and adopt proven strategies that drive results.

Encouragement and Next Steps

Embarking on an SEO journey can feel overwhelming at first, but remember that every step you take is a move towards greater visibility and success for your accounting firm. Whether you're a solo practitioner just getting started or a larger firm looking to refine your strategy, SEO has the potential to transform your online presence and help you reach new heights.

Encouragement:
  - Start Small: You don't need to implement everything at once. Begin with the basics, such as optimizing your website's content and meta tags, then gradually expand your efforts to include more advanced tactics like link building and content marketing.
  - Be Patient: SEO is a long-term investment, and it can take time to see

significant results. Stay consistent, monitor your progress, and keep refining your approach. Over time, your efforts will pay off.

- Celebrate Small Wins: Celebrate milestones along the way, whether it's a rise in your rankings, an increase in organic traffic, or positive feedback from a client who found you online. These small victories are indicators of your growing success.

Next Steps:
1. Conduct an SEO Audit: If you haven't already, perform a comprehensive SEO audit of your website. Identify strengths, weaknesses, and areas for improvement. Use this audit as the foundation for your ongoing SEO strategy.
2. Set Clear Goals: Define your SEO goals based on your business objectives. Whether it's increasing traffic, boosting lead generation, or improving local visibility, having clear goals will guide your efforts and keep you focused.
3. Develop a Content Plan: Plan out your content strategy for the next 6-12 months. Identify key topics that align with your services and target audience, and create a content calendar to ensure consistent publishing.
4. Monitor and Adjust: Regularly track your SEO performance and make data-driven adjustments. SEO is not static; it's about continuous improvement and adapting to new challenges and opportunities.

Final Tips for SEO Success in Accounting

To conclude, here are some final tips to help you achieve SEO success in the accounting industry:

1. Focus on Quality Over Quantity: Quality content, back links, and user experience should always take precedence over quantity. A few well-placed, high-quality back links are more valuable than numerous low-quality ones, and comprehensive, informative content will always outperform thin, keyword-stuffed pages.

2. Prioritize User Experience: Search engines are increasingly focusing on

user experience as a ranking factor. Ensure your website is easy to navigate, loads quickly, and provides a seamless experience across all devices. A positive user experience not only boosts your SEO but also encourages visitors to stay longer and engage more with your content.

3. Leverage Local SEO: For accounting firms, local SEO is often a key driver of new business. Optimize your Google My Business profile, encourage client reviews, and focus on location-specific keywords to enhance your local visibility.

4. Stay Ethical with Your SEO Practices: Avoid black-hat SEO tactics like keyword stuffing, cloaking, or buying back links. These practices may offer short-term gains but can lead to penalties from search engines, damaging your rankings and reputation in the long run.

5. Build Relationships: Networking with other professionals in the accounting industry can lead to valuable back links, guest posting opportunities, and collaborations. Building relationships with other reputable businesses, bloggers, and influences in your field can also help boost your site's authority and broaden your reach.

6. Optimize for Mobile: With the growing number of users accessing the internet via mobile devices, having a mobile-optimized website is no longer optional. Ensure your site is responsive, loads quickly on mobile devices, and offers an intuitive navigation experience to keep mobile users engaged.

7. Use Structured Data Markup: Implementing structured data (schema markup) helps search engines better understand your content and can improve your chances of appearing in rich snippets. This not only increases your visibility in search results but also enhances your click-through rates.

8. Monitor Competitor Strategies: Keep an eye on what your competitors are doing in terms of SEO. Use tools like Ahrefs or SEMrush to analyze their

keywords, back links, and content strategies. Learning from your competitors can provide insights into what's working well in your industry and help you identify opportunities to differentiate yourself.

9. Encourage and Showcase Client Reviews: Positive client reviews can significantly impact your online reputation and influence potential clients. Encourage satisfied clients to leave reviews on platforms like Google My Business, Yelp, and other review sites. Displaying these reviews prominently on your website can build trust and credibility with prospective clients.

10. Stay Consistent and Persistent: SEO is an ongoing effort that requires consistency and persistence. Regularly update your content, monitor your performance, and make adjustments as needed. Stay committed to your SEO strategy, even when results aren't immediate, and over time, you'll see the benefits of your hard work.

Final Thoughts

SEO is a powerful and essential tool for accounting firms in today's digital age. By mastering the basics, continuously learning, and staying committed to best practices, you can significantly improve your online presence and attract the right clients to your business.

Remember, SEO success doesn't happen overnight. It's a marathon, not a sprint, requiring dedication, flexibility, and a willingness to adapt to changes in the digital landscape. With a strong, ongoing SEO strategy, you can ensure your accounting firm remains visible, relevant, and competitive for years to come.

Start with the fundamentals, set clear goals, and build your SEO efforts incrementally. Use the insights and strategies shared in this guide as a road map, and don't hesitate to seek professional guidance if needed. With persistence, strategic planning, and a focus on providing value to your audience, you can achieve lasting SEO success and drive meaningful growth for your accounting practice.

www.ingramcontent.com/pod-product-compliance
Lightning Source LLC
Chambersburg PA
CBHW050306230526
45471CB00005B/2039